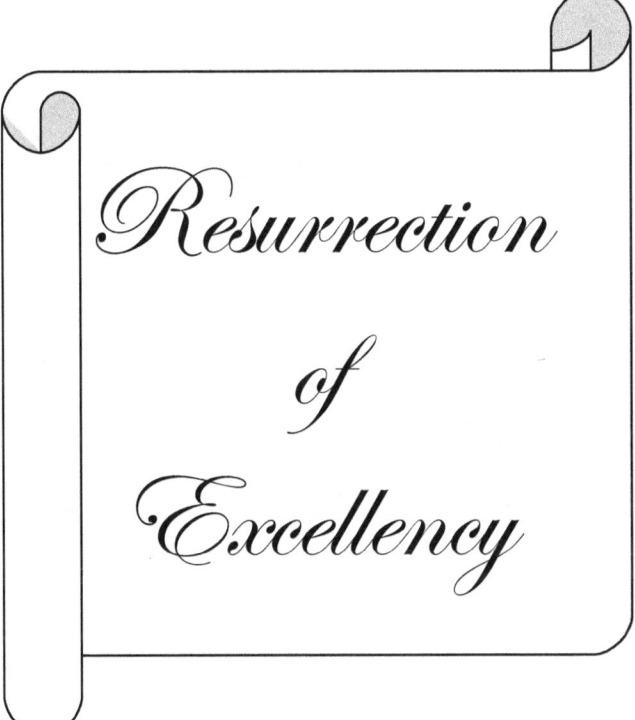

Resurrection of Excellency

Written by Darold Edwards

Copyright © 2007 Darold F. Edwards
Revised September 2011
Editing Assistance by MyKeyWeb.com

Resurrection of Excellency

Table of Contents:

i.	General Introduction	5
ii.	Acknowledgment	15
iii.	Preface	19
iv.	ROE Introduction	23
I.	Resurrection of Excellence	27
II.	The Journey	37
III.	Questions	45
IV.	The Excellency Within	69
V.	State of the Heart	81
VI.	Basic Values	97
VII.	Personal Observation	113
VIII.	One Nation, Under God	121
IX.	Bible Consciousness	145

A General Introduction to
The Works of
Darold Edwards

I would like to begin this introduction of myself and my writings with a greeting to all who are gracious enough to take the time to read my writings and join me in this journey of Bible exploration and study. This greeting is found in **[2 Peter 1: 2], "Grace and peace be multiplied to you through the knowledge of God, and of Jesus our Lord"**. In **[Galatians 2: 6] Paul writes of people "who added nothing to me"**. It is my desire and prayer that these writings will add much to you in your Bible explorations and enrichment of life.

Let me introduce myself to you. It is very likely you have never heard of me but that is alright, as I have never heard of the vast majority of you, but, I know you are out there somewhere in our big wide world that seems to be getting smaller with a disturbing amount of consistency. At the present time I am 75 years old, and like most of everything else in this world, my age is subject to constant change. My wife of 52, going on 53 years of marriage, Patricia, is a very wonderful person who has had the grace to put up with me these many years gone by and has been a constant source of help, strength, and encouragement to me; with a little challenge thrown in from time to time to help keep life interesting. But having no complaints, I am looking forward to a continuation of our life together, at least for some time to come. We have our home in Albany, Oregon, raised 3 children there and have grandchildren and great grandchildren.

After a privileged time as a child and young person under the care and guidance of some very wonderful loving parents, I proceeded on to adulthood with an average course of life doing some things I should and some that I shouldn't. My specific vocation, after various jobs, was about 42 years as an electrician which was enjoyed very much. In the latter portion of this time I was able and blessed to assist in many church construction jobs as an electrician. There came a time, however, that my body convinced me it was time to seek other easier things to do. After that career ran its course and was fading into the sunset, I was led into an interest in writing, which is where I am today and will probably be for the remainder of my time on this earth. I am enjoying it with much satisfaction, and what you see here is among the beginnings of it. I hope you will blessed by it.

My main interest and priority is and has been in pursuit of Biblical study and knowledge for several years. As I get an ever increasing **"vision of the value"** of such study and exploration, the interest and priority increases accordingly. This Biblical knowledge with its provision of life and life more abundantly through Jesus Christ our Lord, indeed has become my life with its great and perfect peace with joy unspeakable and full of glory. What a blessed state of being to enjoy an unending hope and blessed assurance of a future that extends from today on to and including eternity.

Not being very impressed with humanity in its general condition and what it has done to this world God has provided for it, much of my writings will be addressing this issue and whose responsible for such a degraded condition as this world is in, including our "Land of the Free and the Home of the Brave". You may not agree with me in some of my views and interpretations, but it is only important that you be in agreement with Jesus. Some of the positions I take on traditional Bible interpretations will be somewhat controversial, maybe even viewed as heretical by some, but will certainly provide reason for some new exploration of thinking and thought. God tells us in **[Isaiah 55: 8-9], "My thoughts are not your thoughts, neither are my ways your ways, saith the Lord. For as the heavens are higher than the earth, so are my ways higher than your ways, and my thoughts than your thoughts"**.

So as we re-explore some of these old traditional truths and absolutes of God's Word that have brought life, strength, stability, and comfort to all who embrace them, lets keep our minds open to other additional concepts, original ideas, thoughts and ways that are a part of the expanse between where we are today and where God is calling us to be. I do not believe, that in the fullness of God's greatness, man has reached the end of all God has for us to think about either in the knowledge we are to gain or in the development of our mental capabilities. Much education and knowledge lay before us yet to be attained to. Once again, it is not important that you agree with me, but don't get caught in disagreement with God and his Word, that is a fatal mistake that is much to prevalent in our world today.

My writings are not meant to be entertaining, though a bit of mirth from time to time is acceptable. Yet encouragement and inspiration for meditation and diligent, committed study for spiritual growth and development resulting in intimate fellowship and relationship with God and our Saviour and Lord Jesus Christ is, and remains, the priority. I will be using some words that may offend some but are meant to describe some very apparent conditions that are alive and more sick than well, yet thriving and somewhat destructive, in humanity. God is much more of a gentleman than I am and limits his language to words such as fool, fools, and foolishness. I get a little rougher in my references to mankind and use words such as stupid, idiotic, ignorance etc.

Please understand I have nothing against people, only against the conditions listed above, stupidity, idiocy, and ignorance, etc, that humanity has such an overwhelming desire to wallow and remain in to the degradation of themselves, their societies, and nations, when God, in his love, has given us the remedy for deliverance from such nonsense. To refuse, or neglect, to avail oneself of what God has made available for deliverance from sin and its results in itself, puts a persons intelligence in question.

You are certainly welcome to disagree with me and raise an argument in protest if you wish, however, just a little understanding of the condition our nation is in and how it arrived at this state of demise from the abominations of sin and iniquity of its inhabitants should settle the argument and any questions about it once and for all.

I do hope to wake many minds that have gone to sleep to the challenge of some new in-depth thought that will project them into new ways of life and living where **"the heart is diligently kept, clean, and guarded" [Proverbs 4:23], the mind and spirit are renewed, [Romans 12: 2; Psalms 51:10], and the soul prospers" [3 John: 2].** If we continue to think the way we've always thought, we'll continue to get what we've always got. The way humanity is digressing, we cannot afford to continue along that road of demented mentality, either as individuals or as a nation.

It is my intention that other books will be written as the inspiration to do so presents itself. Several others are already in the works, all dealing with Biblical truths as they relate to the problems and dilemmas of our present day and time; all based on man's disobedience and rebellion against God. This has been the story down through the ages and has only intensified as the population of man has increased, **[Hosea 4: 7], "As they**

were increased, so they sinned against me: therefore I will change their glory into shame". It is this increase in intensity of disobedience, rebellion, sin, iniquity, etc, etc, call it what you will, that has proven so disastrous to mankind, that prompts referral to the conditions of stupidity, idiocy, and ignorance with which man has so chosen to characterize himself.

It is the overabundance of these things that has brought such confusion and chaos to our nation and indeed the world. We could work our way through some of it, but when it became the norm of mankind's mentality and conduct, we have become overwhelmed by it, and can no longer see a light at the end of the tunnel, so to speak. The problems have not changed thru the ages, but remain internal, in the mentalities of some of **"our own countrymen"** who have formed alliances against the Bible, its teachings, and those who teach it. As a result, our leaders are frustrated, the news media is frustrated, and consequently the people are driven to frustration, and confusion seems to reign supreme, especially in the ranks of the people who have rejected God's word of truth and absolutes.

I will refrain from opening any argument as to whether or not the redeemed community of Christ are any better than the unsaved, as **[John 3: 16]** points out that Christ died for all, of which we were all qualified as ungodly, **[Romans 3: 23], " For all have sinned and come short of the glory of God".** I am willing to leave that distinction between the saved and unsaved up to God as he separates the sheep from the goats, as who qualifies as a sheep versus a goat is entirely up to him, **[Matthew 25: 32].** In the meantime, however we might consider **[Acts 10: 34-35]** as a point of interest and consideration by those who have eyes to see, ears to hear, and minds that are capable of comprehension and at least a little bit of understanding; **"Then Peter open his mouth and said, of a truth I perceive that God is no respecter of persons: BUT in** every nation he that feareth him, and worketh righteousness, is accepted with him".

Having favor with God through meeting his Biblical directed requirements for such favor, and being accepted with him is a very comforting, and intelligent, position to be in. You may well get away with disagreeing with me, but to disagree with God will have some eternal devastating affects: I would suggest a path more in line with God's choosing. I would offer **[Deuteronomy 30: 19]** for intense consideration and study for beginners and as a refresher for the more advanced students, or just readers, of the bible.

Please don't get me wrong: I am not down on America, only the stupidity and ignorance that is bringing about her ruin, and the idiots that promote and practice it; which is all within their "rights" of course. God created us to be intelligent beings, however, Adam cast that aside when he abdicated his dominion authority to Satan in the Garden of Eden, and man has been abdicating every since. Retained and exercised Godly intelligence would prevent the things that are bringing ruination, shame, and disgrace on our beloved America, but Godly intelligence and common sense seem to be non-existent in our nation these days along with other things mentioned in the Bible that are commensurate with righteous and holiness.

The question of, who is to blame, should prompt some interesting discussion and dialogue. Who knows, during the process, we might even discover the solution to many of our problems. As Christians, that should already be quite apparent. **[Isaiah 5: 24], "Therefore as the fire devoureth the stubble, and the flame consumeth the chaff, so their root shall be as rottenness, and their flower shall go up as the dust: BECAUSE they have cast away the law of the Lord of hosts, and despised the word of the Holy One of Israel".** The first portion of this scripture gives us a fair description of America if we don't get our spiritual act together. The latter portion gives us the result of excommunicating God and His Word by such things as "the separation of the church and state".

Then we have the remedy, **[Mark 1: 15], "Repent and believe the gospel unto diligent obedience.** This is a repeat of **[2 Chronicles 7: 14], "If my people, which are called by my name, shall humble themselves, and pray, and seek my face, and turn from their wicked ways;** *then* **I will hear from heaven, and will forgive their sin, and will heal their land".** There are a few more words used to emphasize this repentance essential, but the message is the same. **[Deuteronomy 28]** gives a very graphic difference between the people who dwell on the **"If thou wilt hearken diligently"** side of God's directions versus the unrepentant, **"If thou wilt not hearken diligently"** side in rebellion and disobedience. Consider this carefully.

Lacking the extended education that many of today's authors have, you may find my writings a bit rough around the edges for which I make no apology. This could prove an advantage in some ways as I don't have some things to unlearn as I progress and move ahead in my own studies. However, if we all stay with the same Bible for the purpose of unity, **[John 17],** and, to put in today's vernacular, "being on the same page", worshipping and serving the same God, creator of heaven and earth, the God of Israel, and diligently adhering to His counsel, we should remain fairly accurate as we progress, **"seated together in heavenly places in Christ", [Ephesians 2: 4-10],** continuing toward our eternal destiny of the kingdom of heaven while **[Deuteronomy 28: 47], "serving the Lord our God with joyfulness, and with gladness of heart for the abundance of all things".**

Though it seems that I may ramble a bit from time to time, it is my intention, whether I succeed or not, to present the readers with some Biblical truths and challenges they can get their "spiritual teeth into" for the purpose of growth, and development that they can apply toward Christian maturity, providing they are interested in doing so. If they are not so inclined, it is my prayer that some of these writings will induce enough curiosity to provide a challenge to compel them to additional studies, with my own writings and a multitude of others that are available to them. Let me challenge you to choose the books you read, and study, with wisdom and discretion, selecting only those that **"add something to you"** in the way of developing a Biblical, Christ like character, personality and attitude, **"with the Word of God dwelling in you richly", [Colossians 3: 15-17], vs. 16.**

You may find an occasional word misspelled for which I do apologize. Nevertheless, my main concern is that it is not spelled so badly that it fails to contribute constructively to the message it is intended to convey. Allow me to assume my readers will have enough grace to overlook my errors and enough intelligence to get over the rough spots and around the chuck holes and capture the essence of these writings. May God richly bless you as you graciously walk with me through my efforts to present God's truth and absolutes to you for counsel, guidance, and direction unto life and life more abundantly, giving glory, honor, and pleasure, to God, magnifying our Saviour Jesus, and edifying the body of Christ.

Although I am a fan of the Kings James Version, which I will use in the majority of my writing, I will not hesitate to refer to other Versions from time to time as occasionally I will find a word or phrase that seems more preferable to what needs to be said in order to get a better understanding of the message being given. An attempt will be made to identify the use of these various scriptures from the different versions with an explanation of why they are being used in preference to the K.J.V. By doing this it is hoped we can "stay on the same page".

You will notice the use of much scripture throughout my writing with several scriptures being used many times in various situations. You may criticize this as redundancy if you wish. We were all born critics and man has developed it to a fine art, whether it be constructive or destructive, which it is in most cases as man has only to allow his nature to take its natural course to do this. However, what some may view as redundancy in the often use and application of Biblical truths, I simply see as **"emphasis"** to be diligently applied as needed substance for Christian character and development in all our lives. May God give you additional understanding of his word every time you come into contact with it. May it be often and consistent; for emphasis and effect, of course.

As a conclusion to this introduction, allow me once again to go to the scriptures, **[Hebrews 13: 20-21], "Now the God of peace, that brought again from the dead our Lord Jesus, that great shepherd of the sheep, through the everlasting covenant, Make you perfect in every good work to do his will, working in you that which is well pleasing in his sight, through Jesus Christ; to whom be glory for ever and ever. Amen.** I look forward to meeting you in heaven, and possibly before.

Sincerely, in God's love
Darold F. Edwards

NOTES

ACKNOWLEDGMENTS

I would like to thank the people who from the very beginning as a novice writer were kind enough to read some of my earliest efforts and gave me some very encouraging reviews. First of course I would like to thank God for guiding me into writing. It has become a real Godsend to me and has provided direction and purpose for me at a time when otherwise, retirement could have been very trying. I need purpose in my life and writing of the nature you will see in these books gave me that. During my electrical career when I was able to help build some material churches, I thought that someday I would like to assist in building the spiritual church in the hearts and lives of people. God has opened the door to do that through writing for which I wish to express my soul depth gratitude.

Next, many heartfelt thanks to my dear wife Pat for encouraging me in everything along the way in our life together, what a strength and help she has been to me. Susan Canfield was one of the first, who has been very encouraging from the start. She also trims our Schnauzer, Max, which is another big help. This doesn't really have anything to do with my writing except it provides opportunity to visit with Susan from time to time to get additional input on the writing; she is always encouraging. Susan has been very helpful and encouraging in her comments and friendship. Thank you Susan.

Then there is Jock and Karen Elliot, some dear Christian friends who along with their family we have been blessed to know for many reasons including their encouragement in writing. Karen is also a great cook, which is another real advantage to knowing the right people, and I have been much blessed in this area by her talent. My son Myke is of an absolute necessity and blessing as he is my computer expert along with being my son and a very dear friend. I couldn't do this without him. Thanks Myke, for your ever patient and loving assistance along the way.

Then there is my dear friend and brother in the Lord, Clarence Parker, who comes over a couple of times a week just to talk, discuss, study Bible, and add his encouragement to me in my writing efforts. His comments are extremely uplifting and helpful. He also benefits from Karen's cooking, as do all who attend the Elliot's prayer meetings. What a great blessing and strength he is. Thank you my brother for standing alongside me during my writing struggles. Another dear friend, Nancy Gerling, has read some of my writings and has copies of my first efforts to have books published. She has always been extremely uplifting with her input concerning my writing. Many thanks to you, Nancy.

There are others that have added much to me with their encouraging comments about my works which are much appreciated. May God's blessings be upon them and may his presence fill their hearts and lives. May God's blessings also be added to you who are gracious enough to become a part of my reading public; let us study God's word together as he quickens us together in Christ, raises us up together, and makes us to sit together in heavenly places in Christ Jesus our Lord and Saviour, these places being made heavenly because of His presence, wherever that may be. May God's divine love abound in our hearts toward one another. Indeed; we do become a part of each other as we are a part of the body of Christ our Lord.

A little over a year ago as I was looking through a magazine advertising for a Restore America event, I run across another page where someone made the statement, **"How much**

information do we need before we get out of the boat and walk on the water". Whoever that person is, and wherever he may be, I would like to thank him for impacting my life with that inspirational word. Stepping out in faith and writing as I feel led of the Lord in my efforts is my way of walking on the water.

Your efforts are probably of a different calling than mine, but yet of the divine nature. May we blend our efforts and lives together in the unity Jesus prayed for in **John 17** for God's glory, honor, and pleasure. Come, walk with me as we journey along together with the multitudes who will join with us, as we all walk and sit together **"in heavenly places",** inspiring each other as Jesus inspires us all. **To God be the glory forever and ever, Amen.**

NOTES

PREFACE

[Ecclesiastes 12: 11-12], "The words of the wise are as goads, and as nails fastened by the masters of the assemblies, which are given from one Shepard. And further, by these, my son, be admonished: of making many books there is no end; and much study is a weariness to the flesh". Much study demands considerable self discipline, diligence and determination, and a lot of invested time, whereas simply reading for the enjoyment of what is being read, or other lesser purposes, without the element of **"study to show thyself approved unto God", [2 Timothy 2: 15],** tends to a great waste of time.

However, such is not the case if a time of relaxation from business or other things that tend to stress is needed, and reading a good book that is a "no brainer" may be just the ticket. Unfortunately this becomes the norm for many people. As a result many books that neither contribute anything of value and adding nothing constructive to the reader, are in great abundance and offer no challenge for growth and development. Consequently no study is required that would demand thought and concentration, so these books are read in pursuit of nothing, then put aside in favor of another "nothing" book or maybe just watching soap operas on T.V. or the equivalent in "nothing". Habits are thus formed with the result being wasted time and life.

Allow me to express extreme caution in the selection of your reading material as your reading is a direct input into the content of your mind and contributes heavily to "the abundance of your heart". So once again I say, proceed with wisdom, knowledge, understanding, and caution, applying some intelligence and plain common sense along the way, **[Proverbs 4: 23], "Keeping thy heart with all diligence; for out of it are the issues of life". [Proverbs 2: 11], "Discretion shall preserve thee; understanding shall keep thee".**

If we do not endeavor to establish our values and standards according to God's values and standards, we will exist in error continually without the life God has made available to us through Jesus Christ. It is with this in mind that I have set out to produce this work concerning the "RESURRECTION OF EXCELLENCY", to challenge the readers, whoever or wherever they may be: to look inside themselves and ask intelligent questions about their being, who they are, what they are, how they came to be, their purpose, and what their eternal destiny is, and what it is comprised of and by God's design. I find it very enlightening to realize I have by "intelligent design" been created as a very special and unique being instead as a blob of something left to chance as claimed by some who are also willing to risk their eternal destiny with their continuing low level of an unchallenged demented mentality.

Don't think me uncaring and insensitive to others because I use words such as stupidity, idiocy, and ignorant at times. We have all been there and if we are not careful and conscientious about our Christian training, have a tendency to revert back to old habits from time to time. I have nothing against man; only against the inadequate mentalities they have chosen to victimize themselves with. Even as Christians, former erroneous habits and desires, at times even with God's assistance, are hard to shake and it takes time, perseverance and diligence to cast them aside and grow out of them. They may or may not be classified as sin in all cases, but regardless consist of things that do not **"please the Lord," [John 8: 29], or "accompany salvation," [Hebrews 6: 9].** But in any event we need to **[2 Timothy 2: 15], "Study to show ourselves approved unto God, workmen** that needeth not to be ashamed, rightly dividing the word of truth." This involves the extensive effort of **[Romans 12: 2] "being transformed by the renewing of the mind", "exercising thyself unto Godliness", [1 Timothy 4: 7].**

The displacing of these life destroying discrepancies will only be accomplished with the diligent study and input of God's Word. These are just simply some destructive traits of humanity that if not addressed and dealt with according to God's counsel, will continue to plague their unsuspecting, unknowledgeable victims regardless of whether or not they are saved. The devil is not choosey who he victimizes and he will use any method at his disposal to re-devour anyone who becomes negligent in the **"keeping of the heart with all diligence", [Proverbs 4: 23].** Remember, as a Christian, you are his prime target, you are his priority. All others are already devoured. Such is the result of disregarding God's counsel and direction to **"choose life and blessing rather than death and cursing" [Deuteronomy 30: 19].**

I have had to reject the traditional terminology of "sinner saved by grace" in favor of **"a new creature in Christ, saved by Grace", [2 Corinthians 5: 17].** The reason for this was because the term "sinner" was not conducive to being **[1 John 1: 7-9], "forgiven of sin and cleansed from all unrighteousness by the blood of Jesus."** This is an insult to the power of the blood of Jesus to thoroughly cleanse from sin and unrighteousness in the name of Jesus for complete cleansing, forgiveness, deliverance and reconciliation. All this of course, is based on the condition of genuine, soul depth, repentance of sin and a commitment to **"fear [reverence] the Lord and work righteousness" [Acts 10: 35], serving the Lord with joyfulness and with gladness of heart, for the abundance of all things, [Deuteronomy 28: 47].** You may not agree with me on this issue and that's not important. Just be in agreement with God. It's his word that counts, not mine.

After all that God has done for us through Jesus Christ our Lord and Saviour in obtaining the **"divine nature of God through his great and precious promises", [2 Peter 1:2 -4],** it seemed that the title and name of "sinner" had some rather antagonistic and invasive qualities and connotations about it that never belonged nor fit in well with being "a new creature in Christ saved by grace". The term "sinner" always suggested being stuck in a rut with no incentive to move on, whereas the new distinction and a new attitude concerning being "a new creature in Christ" provides a glorious challenge to, **[1 Peter 1: 13], "Gird up the loins of our [spiritual] minds"** and, **[Hebrews 6: 1-3], "go on unto perfection"**, to the **[Job 4: 21], "Resurrection of the Excellency" which is in you, lest ye die, even without wisdom."**

iv. **ROE INTRODUCTION**

The idea of this **"excellency"**, worded as such in the **KJV** in this verse is taken from **[JOB 4:20-21]**, where Eliphaz, the Temanite, one of Job's friends who came to comfort Job in his distress was telling of a vision he had of a spirit that appeared to him in the night. This scripture in other versions of the Bible refer to **"their tent cords being plucked or pulled up within them"**, giving a totally different terminology. However, if you are familiar with tent camping and know the importance of the combination of solidly driven tent pegs and tight tent ropes you can recognize the value of the support mechanism of the matter of "excellency" as the supporting strength for the stability of the structure dependant on the tent ropes and pegs being the excellency referred to here; especially if a storm happens to come up in the middle of the night. This should give us all an understanding of the connection regardless of the Bible version being used. It would be pointless to enter into a discussion of the origin of this spirit as all we would get is different opinions. We have enough of those to create mountains of confusion already. I would simply call attention to what the spirit had to say about this **"them that dwell in houses of clay", verse 19,** man, formed by God out of the dust of the ground, **[Genesis 2:7]**.

What he had to say about this man creature pretty well fits his profile, so I had to conclude this spirit as sent of God to reveal some things of extreme interest and importance to man that will assist us in maturing in Christ and attaining to the realization of the presence of this internally designed God like created **"excellency which is in them"**. This depends on our taking the time and exerting the effort needed to, **[2 Timothy 2:15]** **"Study to show thyself approved unto God, a**

workman that needeth not to be ashamed, rightly dividing the word of truth. This little word **"if"**, as a fork in the road of life, seems to be a bit of a stumbling block to many on their road to maturity in Christ. Possibly in a time of meditation, **if** a person would, they could. **If** they would exercise themselves to, get a "vision of the value" of intimacy with God, they would be able to avoid this stumbling block with ease in their pursuit of **"the things that always please God" [John 8:29]. [Deu. 28]**

May I assure you, one and all, the rewards are well worth the effort. There are many things that please God and all of them come by way of the counsel of his word. In **[1 Timothy 4:7]** we are commanded to **"refuse profane** [look this up in your dictionary and study it to get a good understanding of its various meanings and adverse effects it has on a persons life] **and old wives fables, and exercise thyself rather unto Godliness."** Exercising ourselves unto Godliness presents a full time challenge and won't be accomplished without some intense study and thought, **"meditation"**.

Until Christians finally arrive at the place of manifesting the Christ-like attitude of **[John 4:34]** in serving God in obedience, we will not accomplish our life's purpose. **"Jesus saith unto them, my meat,** [my entire sustenance, my life, my purpose], **is to do the will of him who sent me, and to finish his work".** This includes the developing of a love, a desire and appreciation of God's abundance and **[Colossians 3:2], "setting your [entire] affection on things above, [that proceed from the heart of God] not on things on the earth".** How do these *"things above"* compare to the *"things that accompany salvation"* **[Hebrews 6:9]**? How do they compare with Jesus' example of **[John 8:29] "doing always those things that please him"** that are the "offspring" of correct, Biblical renewed mind thinking and thoughts?

These thoughts, because they are Bible conditioned thoughts are commensurate with God's thoughts, thus our **"doing always those things that please him"** are commensurate with his ways. In this developmental process, our intimacy with God is constantly being strengthened and enriched. It involves **[Psalms 1:2; 119:165], loving and delighting in his word, studying and meditating in it day and night and [Colossians 3:17], "And whatsoever ye do in word or deed do all in the name of the Lord Jesus, giving thanks to God and the Father by him".** **[1 Corinthians 10:31], "Whether ye therefore eat or drink, or whatsoever ye do, do all to the glory of God".**

My purpose, my desire, my prayer, is that this book will cause you to want to know more about this "excellency" that is in you, unacknowledged, unknown, thus unexplored, neglected, and dormant. Ask yourself these questions about it and dig for the answers.

Where did it come from?

What is it?

What is its purpose?

Of what does it consist?

Why haven't I known about it?

Of what benefit is it to me?

Why is it in a dormant state and condition?

Can it be dominate in my life; If so, how?

These and other questions that are sure to arise I hope to answer, and help you answer here in this writing as we all follow the teaching and counseling of the Holy Spirit through God's word, our textbook through this school of thought. Join me now as we set out on this journey to explore and enjoy this **"Resurrection of the Excellency"** that is in you, awaiting your discovery.

May God bless and guide us on our "journey", as we learn and grow together, in heavenly places in Christ, [Ephesians 2:4-10].

NOTES

_____
_____
_____
_____
_____
_____
_____
_____
_____
_____
_____
_____
_____
_____
_____

I. RESURRECTION OF EXCELLENCE

It is out of a deep sense of concern for my Christian family, whomever and wherever they might be, and the iniquity that is making such inroads into the church, as well as society, that I feel a necessity to produce this work concerning a resurrection that is never spoken of as such, but found throughout the Bible by the use of other words. Maybe the meaning of both words in the title, *"resurrection" and "excellency"*, if understood better, would assist in spotting these other phrases and terms that convey a resurrection concept, many of which are direct commands from the Lord to do so.

First let's take a look at "resurrection". Resurrection: to rise again, revive, a rising from the dead or, a [*state of deadness or being dormant*], coming or bringing back to life; a coming back into notice, practice, use, etc.; restoration or revival as of old customs, principles, etc. This particular work is concerned with the old Biblical customs and principles that reproduce a Christ character, building life from a dead or dormant state of being. Generally speaking, resurrection has to do with the "bringing back to life of dead [bodies]".

There are, however, some things that need to be "resurrected", revived, or as they are spoken of in **[Revelations 3]**, concerning the church of Sardis. **Verse 1-3, "I know thy works, that thou hast a name that thou livest, and are dead. Vs. 2 be watchful, and strengthen the things which remain, that are [in their death throes] ready to die: for I have not found thy works perfect before God".** These are the things that remain; struggling for one last breath of life, after everything else is dead. There is a command from God here to "be watchful [it would seem that "diligence" is one of the things already dead] and strengthen [revive, renew, resurge, or resurrect] the things that are about to die" [in a state of deadness], so close to death they qualify for "resurrection".

There is at the present time movements in concern for our nations spiritual condition that are under way for the "Restoring or Renewing of America" to a time when people, definitely including her leaders, seemed to be much more aware of the need for God's providential guidance and counsel in her affairs. These movements and efforts are being made out of a very apparent need for America and her Christian, Biblical beginning and heritage to be resurrected and renewed.

Only the Bible, God's Word, the true, accurate, living and authoritative "Law of the Land" contains the power to change men's hearts toward the righteousness and holiness needed to produce the outward conduct and ways that the exterior laws of man have attempted to do, but have failed miserably. There is certainly a need for the **"Resurrection of God's Excellence"** in the hearts, minds and lives of humanity, and most assuredly in the hearts and minds of those to whom the over all well being of the nation and it's people have been entrusted.

In [**2 Chronicles 7:14**] we find another example of a need for a "resurrection". This verse is quoted and used but it seems never heeded, nor initiated. Is it because the people have failed in their mental capacities to grasp the awful result of their violation of heeding God's counsel? At least we don't see much evidence of it being taken seriously in this world today, including America. **"If my people, which are called by my name, shall humble themselves, and pray, and seek my face, and turn from their wicked ways; then will I hear from heaven, and will forgive their sin, and will heal their land"**.

Question! Would you consider **"wicked ways"** to include refusing and neglecting the **"renewing of the mind" unto Godliness as a violation [Romans 12:2],** a part of this requirement? Will it suffice to consider this as **"under grace"** and then neglect it; or consider it as direct command and law, or principle, in the **"working of righteousness, [Acts 10:34-35],** and be obedient to it? Which way will produce benefits and rewards and please God? The first part of this verse is a strong suggestion from God concerning our part we are to play in this. Shall we refer to it as a "resurrection" of our land, through the "resurrection of excellence" in the people by way of submission and willing obedience to God?

God being who and what he is, it would be wise to take his simple suggestions as commands. Contingent on our following his "suggestions or commands, whichever way you wish to consider them, is his promise to **"hear from heaven, forgive their sin, and heal the land".** Hear, forgive, heal, to bring back to health with the ability to function properly as intended; it sounds amazingly like a "resurrection" to me.

"If my people shall humble themselves, pray, seek my face, and turn from their wicked ways"; this sounds like **"repentance", [Mark 1:15].** Let's condense all this down to "IF" people will repent, I will resurrect them and their land from death unto life". **[John 5:24],** Jesus is speaking here and says; **"Verily, verily, I say unto you, he that heareth my word, and believeth on him that sent me, hath everlasting life, and shall not come into condemnation; but is passed from death unto life.** Again, in **[1 John 3:14]; "We know that we have passed from death unto life, because we love the brethren. He that loveth not his brother abideth in death",** remains un-resurrected, in a state of spiritual deadness.

All of these examples, situations, and conditions pertain to a state of spiritual "deadness" in people's lives, a being separated from God and in need of a spiritual resurrection, or a **"resurrection of spiritual excellence"**. This is not, and I realize this, the bodily resurrection spoken of to come in the future concerning those who have "died in Christ;" however, if you choose to not take part in this "spiritual resurrection", this repentance of sin and being born again, saved, washed in the blood of Jesus, don't expect to be resurrected to the same "physical" resurrection as awaits the saints of the most high God.

Now let's consider this **"excellency that is in them" that goes away and they perish, even without wisdom.** What is this "excellency" and of what does it consist? It is impossible, in this world, with our finite minds to ever get a complete understanding of this when considering the magnitude of the greatness and majesty of God. We could have much dialogue and discussion about this subject, which should provide at least some inspiration for interested persons, but would never really discover the fullness of it.

We can, however, glean sufficient information, inspiration, and revelation from our study, discussions and whatever Biblical input we embrace to advance us on our journey of discovery and maturity in Christ. In **[Genesis 1:26]** we find that we have been "**made, or created, in the image and likeness of God",** and whoever else he was addressing with the word "us". Generally and it seems to be the general consensus, that it had to be Jesus. I certainly have no argument with this conclusion, but can agree with it wholeheartedly.

It never ceases to amaze me, how that we can read a passage of scripture many times, and then in reading it again, something reaches right out, grabs our attention and won't let go. That's the way this word *"excellency"* came to me **[Job 4:21]** and immediately raised some questions, what is it, where did it come from, where did it originate, why hadn't I heard about it before? If it is indeed, in us, why haven't we known about it?

Many questions come to mind about conditions in these two scriptures as well as about this spirit that seemed to appear to Eliphaz, one of Jobs comforters earlier in verses **12-19**. After reading what this spirit said about **"they who dwell in houses of clay,** man," I concluded this spirit surely must have been a servant of God for it certainly gave some very vivid facts about us, the truth of which is a bit disturbing. It does seem that the individuals referred to in verses **20-21** had never heard about this "excellency", pursued it, and consequently never exercised it in their lives. It has, it seems, remained unacknowledged, unknown and hidden down through the ages.

Perhaps it was hidden; buried under a dominating, ever present teaching about what terrible sinners we are and our need to repent constantly with which we were conditioned that preoccupied our thoughts. However it may have been, and continues to be, our lack of sincere repentance along with in depth study and implementing God's word of truth that indeed sets men free that is causing us so much difficulty and hindering our way to righteousness and Godliness, thus "The Resurrection of Excellency".

Man's mind, such as it is, thus his thinking, thoughts, and ways, is due to a sinful nature and even with God's help has a difficult time fixating on the positive, but instead seems to have an overwhelming propensity for the negative. Thus we are given, in an attempt to counteract this tendency, scriptures such as **[Colossians 3:2]; "Set your affection on things above, not on things on the earth". [Psalms 37:4], "Delight thyself also in the Lord; and he shall give thee the desires of thine** heart". **[Psalms 1: 2]**, **"But his delight is in the law of the Lord; and in his law doth he meditate day and night"**.

This will begin to take shape as we **[2 Timothy 2:15], "Study to show thyself approved unto God, a workman that needeth not to be ashamed, rightly dividing the word of truth"**. This concept of "rightly dividing the word of truth" no doubt leaves some room for error as it is doubtful that in the process of doing this, you will be able to find agreement on many of the interpretations that arise in the "rightly dividing" process. Unfortunately, even in church circles we find sufficient pride that prevents deferring to one another. There seems to be more man-type ego than there is in practice, Christ-like excellency.

This leads us to the need to conform to **[Romans 12:1-2], "I beseech you therefore, brethren, by the mercies of God, that ye present your bodies a living sacrifice, holy, acceptable unto God which is your reasonable service. And be not conformed to this world: but be ye transformed by the renewing of your mind, that ye may prove what is that good, and acceptable, and perfect will of God"**. This is all contributive and lends itself to the awareness of **"the excellency that is in them"**, **[Job 4:21]**, raising our awareness of the sinful things that tend to our destruction, the dissipation of this "excellency" and the loss of Godly wisdom which seems to be a part of it, plus the necessity of executing the God provided and taught corrective measures, **[Mark 1: 15]**.

When my attention was captured by this word, I began to have questions about it. My thoughts were immediately drawn to **[Genesis 1: 26]** where God said, **"Let us make man in our image, after our likeness, and let THEM have dominion over, and over, and over"**. More could be said on the remainder of this verse, as there is, in my estimation, some very important information here as to those whose attention was focused on retaining this "image and likeness". What captured my attention here was not so much the image as the *"likeness"* that was created in us. This likeness contained as part of its qualities, this **"God like excellency" that was initially created "in them"**. What a glorious thing it is to realize that God did not create us as sinners or ever to be sinners, for we were **[Psalms 139:14] "fearfully and wonderfully made, in his image and likeness: marvelous are thy works; and that my soul knoweth right well"**.

Being created in God's image and likeness, with his "excellency" being an intrinsic quality of that likeness will always be a wonder to me. I will never in this world have a perfect understanding of it's significance, but I don't need to in order to be thankful for it, and manifest gratitude for it in living a lifestyle acceptable unto our Lord, **[Acts 10: 35], "But in every nation he that feareth him, and worketh righteousness, is accepted with him"**. The extent of God's love for us is beyond our comprehension.

It would seem that his "image" would have more to do with our physical appearance while his likeness would pertain to the internal portion of our makeup, the spiritual, psychological, intellectual, mentality area where our thinking, thoughts, ideas, concepts, etc, are formed. Surely there is a bridging over between the image and likeness as to our attributes, but at this time the likeness is of the main concern, for in it would be found the "excellency".

This word "excellency" seems to have a presence about it that suggests something majestic, something of greatness that is of immense value above the ordinary, mundane, that we to often settle for. It is certainly something completely opposed to sin, which God hates, **[Proverbs 8:13],** and without a doubt a part of the divine nature of God himself, and to resurrect this "excellency" would definitely qualify us as **partakers of his divine nature" [2 Peter 1:4].** It is important that we study, not only to know him, but to know about him, his nature, character, holiness, righteousness, and his commitment to these and other things we will find are commensurate with these Godly characteristics as we study to show ourselves approved unto God.

Being created, as was his original intention, in his likeness, the more we find out about God the more we will find out about what God intended us to be like and what we can be like if we apply ourselves to his word and his word to our lives; a blending together is definitely implied here, **[John 15:4].** This will be a life long quest with many new wonderful, discoveries and rewards along the way as we progress in his counsel, nurturing, and guidance, being lead and taught by the Holy Spirit all along the journey. **[Isaiah 55:8-9], "For my thoughts are not your thoughts, neither are your ways my ways, saith the Lord. For as the heavens are higher than the earth, so are my ways higher than your ways, and my thoughts than your thoughts.**

Maybe, just maybe, if we apply ourselves we might learn to think more like God thinks so that our ways might become more like his ways. My goodness, wouldn't that be a change? A good place to start would be **"a study and application of those things that accompany salvation", [Hebrews 6:9].** Without these things along with, and including, the **Fruit of the Spirit, [Galatians 5:22-23]** in place and operating in our lives, our souls cannot prosper. **[3 John 1:2], "Beloved, I wish above all things that thou mayest prosper and be in health, even as thy soul prospereth."** May your soul prosper greatly as you live and move and have your being in God, and **"do** always those things that please him," [John 8:29], "Resurrecting the Excellency that is in you."

NOTES

II. THE JOURNEY

Exploration from a general standpoint is faced with many exciting discoveries and possible dangers of various kinds and intensities, depending on where and what you are exploring and the rewards and treasures anticipated. Anticipation can be, and usually is, a great motivator. The exploration that I propose is undoubtedly the most interesting and rewarding that you will ever experience, though to some extent already explored by a few others before us. What you get out of it is strictly up to you.

This particular exploration however, is one that each person must conduct for themselves; preferably in the company and assistance of fellow explorers in the course of their own exploration. The treasures to be found are in many cases found together, and are shared together and with others to give them value and meaning. The only danger involved is to those who choose not to explore the unknown that lies ahead of them, thus denying themselves the knowledge that would avert the destruction that is sure to come without that essential knowledge, **[Hosea 4: 6]**.

It may be difficult for a person to garner the enthusiasm for this exploration without having a pretty good idea of the benefits and rewards to be found and how they will impact their own personal life and the lives of others around them. If peace is an important consideration in life versus turmoil and strife, this journey will assist you in discovering it. If joy and happiness are preferable to sadness, heartache, misery, etc, etc, then this is the journey for you. If deliverance is desired from the death and destruction that is becoming an ever increasing menace in our world and nation, that deliverance is available for you on this journey. These are just a few of the rewards and benefits that await you as we travel along through this life together, exploring the vastness of God's provisions and discovering things beyond our greatest expectations. We must all get a **"Vision of the Value"** of God's glory and majesty he wishes to share with us; the value being life and life more abundantly.

Regardless, we will experience some unknowns of which we may be made aware to a certain extent by some researching of our history and some study of what lay ahead of us depending on the path we choose to take. **[Deuteronomy 30: 19], "I call heaven and earth to record this day against you, that I have set before you life and death, blessing and cursing: Therefore choose life; that both thou and thy seed may live".** The path of life and blessing will require much study and meditation, whereas, the path of death and cursing, requiring nothing of you, is the path you were born on and will remain on until you choose the path of **"life and blessing"**, **"For all have sinned and come short of the glory of God", [Romans 3: 23].** You don't have to choose death and cursing; your already on that trail if you have refused to be "born again" by the Spirit of God into his family, **[Ephesians 2: 4-10].**

Though not entirely unknown by many, this way of life and blessing has nevertheless been rejected and terribly neglected. It is this unknown, the lack of knowledge of which, that is of great danger, **[Hosea 4:6] "My people are destroyed for lack of knowledge".** This first part of **Hosea 4:6** is only an introduction to the rest of the verse that describes the awful result of choosing to remain ignorant of the knowledge required to prevent destruction. For the new explorer there is much left to be examined, studied, explored, and definitely enjoyed as new discoveries are uncovered along the way. Proceed with great expectation of the life and life more abundantly that awaits you. **[Psalms 139: 14]** tells us that **"we are fearfully and wonderfully made"**.

What a marvelous, beyond our comprehension, this God designed creature is, this man, complete with this thing we refer to as a "mind". In some instances it is referred to as **"the heart "or "the inner or new man"**. Regardless of the terminology used, therein is our mentality, our ability to think, develop thoughts, devise concepts, create ideas, design a whole world of goodness and beauty, enjoying and **"doing always those things that please God", [John 8:29].** *This "resurrection of excellency" can only be accomplished by the blending together of the "renewed mind and diligently kept heart" with the Word of God as taught and revealed by the Holy Spirit.* It will take time and determination, but the results and rewards are as wonderful as they are eternal as God re-creates our abilities to please him and give him glory and honour.

Unfortunately man has abused these God given abilities to do good, to instead create evil, thus destroying themselves and others, but for such a time as this, you were created. If this mind, this mentality, has been influenced and conditioned correctly it will tend toward wise intelligent choices. If this mind has, on the other hand, been subjected to adverse contrary conditioning, which is the normal course of this world in general living, child rearing, education, politics, etc., it will naturally gravitate in the direction of that erroneous condition. This is done very easily and at times without thought because it is the way of the evil nature of man, and it takes effort and conscious thought to change, which requires challenge and self discipline few are willing to accept and face. However, you will find it is worth any time and effort you need to expend to accomplish the task.

In our post-modern age of so called relativity, good and evil have been intermingled by the perverted mentalities of the lack and neglect of Biblical input and influence to the point that it is hard to get a grip on what reality is for the purpose of absolute identification of good versus evil that is acceptable, and necessary to all. If people enjoy sin and its pursuit, and they do, though it is sin, they will call it good because it appeals to their feelings and emotions. If on the other hand they are faced with a truth that arouses uncomfortable, undeniable, feelings of guilt that demand correction, because of their sin, they will consider that as evil or bad. This does depend, however, on the extent of the development, or lack thereof, of the **"renewing of the mind", [Romans 12:2]** for the purpose of being transformed out of conformity to this world. **[Isaiah 5:20], "Woe unto them that call evil good, and good evil; that put darkness for light, and light for darkness; that put bitter for sweet, and sweet for bitter."**

It has been said with a great degree of accuracy **"If you continue to think the way you've always thought, you'll continue to get what you've always got."** Considering the condition of America, indeed the world today, and the mentality that has brought us to this condition of calamity and chaos, it is rather disheartening to see such a lack of interest in upgrading and enriching the mentality**, to include the Biblical principles involved and necessary to the production of prosperity of soul and life itself.**

It is equally troubling to think that the problems America is experiencing can be solved with the same sub-level of mentality that has and is causing them, whether it is on a national scale or as an individual. America must raise the bar on her mentality, and reinstate the Biblical principles on which she was founded or continue to struggle under the burden of inadequate, irresponsible thinking and thoughts unto her own destruction.

There are no options to this and neither science nor political correctness, nor anything else outside of God can or will provide solutions.

For the purpose of establishing a solid foundation of absolutes from which to operate and conduct a correct lifestyle of righteousness and holiness that is acceptable to God, we must be anchored in his Word, the Bible as individuals, families, and expanded to governmental and national levels; and still there are no options. **The ages past have not by any means whether it be by philosophy, science, religions, or any other method, produced anything that even begins to compare with God's Word, the Bible as a complete code of conduct and operation of peoples and nations. [Matthew 24:35] "Heaven and earth shall pass away, but my words shall not pass away."** *There can be no doubt, God's word of truth, righteousness, and holiness, in it's design and purpose for the good of humanity qualifies it as the sole* ***"Law of the Land"***.

A word thus unaffected by all the opposition against it certainly qualifies itself as a basis of absolute truth and stability in which we can confidently place our entire being for all things, for all time, including any argument, dialogue, or debate. For indeed it is, **[Acts 17:28], "in him "God" that we live and move and have our being" and find the "Resurrection of Excellency" in his "likeness".**

No other point of view or perspective based on any other source can be considered which can possibly produce life and life more abundantly. None other over ages past have ever qualified themselves as doing so. This is not being intolerant. It is simply being realistic and standing for the truth that over time has proven itself. This is that which must be intelligently chosen to believe in and not compromising it simply because someone wishes, or tries, to intimidate you into doing so regardless of their position or supposed authority, whether it be for political correctness, relativity, diversity, etc.

Biblical correctness supersedes political correctness every time, every place, and under ever circumstance and situation without question or debate. Biblical correctness is based on absolute truth, whereas political correctness is based on whatever those who promote it can get away with regardless of how erroneous or opposed to fact and truth it is.

I am not opposed to political correctness as such, but it is irrelevant in the presence of Biblical truth and correctness. The problem is that we have more people that are ignorant of God's word and are only concerned about what they consider more politically correct than what is Biblically correct. Because of this "lack of knowledge" they strive for political expertise which continues to elude them, but aren't concerned about Biblical expertise and truth, **the truth that sets men and nations free. [Hosea 4:6] "My people are destroyed"……..**

Consequently they continue on, bound in their worldly wisdom with all its deceptions, lies, and half truths, attempting to make it all sound good and acceptable to all concerned. Shakespeare said it well when he said, **"What fools ye mortals be"**! Have a rewarding journey of discovery and attaining to God's truth. **Learn it well, apply it diligently, with zeal and determination; your future and that of your descendents depend on it, in this world and in the world to come. Deu. 4:9; 6:6-7; 11:1; 30:19, Hosea 4:6.**

NOTES

NOTES

III. QUESTIONS

Questions that demand the exploration and development of appropriate, sufficient answers that will satisfy the investigative, curious, not easily satisfied mind, concerning the subjects being considered, will always continue to induce and compel those with questioning minds to search for the truth that will finally satisfy the longing of the soul and bring solace to the spirit. Life is full of questions; some we will never find the answers to; and many that are not worth the effort and time expended on them. These seem to arise more often than not in television talk shows where mundane, shallow, subjects are the only subjects our post-modern society are conditioned to, and able to address, though seldom with any intelligent answers or viable solutions to any significant problems.

There are some very important issues that need addressing, but the talk show mentality, with its anti-God, anti-Bible rhetoric that is so typical of our "if it feels good, do it" society, hasn't shown the depth of intelligence to comprehend the necessity of including God and his Word as essential in their discussions or necessary for remedies to problems. This might lead to the realization that only God has the solutions needed to heal our national and personal dilemmas, which of course would be "politically incorrect". What ever happened to Biblical correctness? Don't we have any "mighty men" of God that are capable of risking everything for the cause of Christ, that are bold enough to speak and declare the Word of God in the face of our enemies, those of "our own countrymen".

We had some founding fathers who put life, families, fame, and fortunes on the line as "mighty men" to establish our nation under God's divine direction. In our modern day "wimpyness" we have allowed the dissenters of righteousness and holiness to destroy what those "mighty men" with their intelligence and courage of yesteryear established for us. Not only do our governing authorities not follow the understanding that God and his Word were essential to the foundation of this nation, they can't even acknowledge the fact that our founding fathers were right for fear of being politically incorrect, suffering at the hands of their spineless colleagues, and offending the anti-God element of our society.

It would be a show of intelligence to not offend God, but be in total agreement with him, and offend those that are opposed to Him. After all, God is calling the shots and his agenda is right on track, whether for blessing for obedience, or cursing for disobedience. The choice is yours.

The vast majority of the dribble on these talk shows is arranged around dialogue and debate that never asks questions that require intelligent answers, only the giving of opinions. Thus the participants never need a way of escape as they avoid getting into a position where their ignorance of viable answers and solutions will be exposed. The most important questions, the ones never asked, are those for which the answers are provided, but unfortunately even though the answers are available, they are rejected by our society and in many cases, if not rejected, miserably neglected. For as the multitudes never ask the right questions of themselves, they never have to attempt to seek the correct answers.

Who, what, and why, are in themselves single words that ask a question concerning those spoken of in **[Job 4:19-21]**. The situations and conditions of those who **"dwell in houses of clay"** are something they should be curious and concerned about. To begin with, who are these that "dwell in houses of clay", that were formed of the dust of the ground? We find our answer in **[Genesis 2:7], "And the Lord God formed man of the dust of the ground, and breathed into his nostrils the breath of life; and man became a living soul",** to dwell in their **"houses of clay".**

Now as to the "why's" concerning these who dwell in these houses of clay, whose foundation is in the dust, vs.19! **Verse 20, "Why" are they destroyed from morning to evening and perish forever? "Why" do they not regard it, or as [Jeremiah 12:11] puts it, "take it to heart".** Why doesn't man simply question; "why" are these things happening to us, and search for the correct answers? Is this man critter so ignorant and unconcerned about himself and his descendents that he simply doesn't give a rip about that which may befall him in his future because of his stupidity? He is going to, one way or another, have a future whether he is concerned or not, whether he likes it or not. That choice is not his; however the choice is his as to what kind of a future he will have and where he is going to spend it.

Seeing as how humanity is the entity so deeply affected by these conditions, and we are all a part of this mass of mankind; why aren't people curious enough to at least consider the possibility that the Bible may just be correct concerning their futures. Why don't they dig for some Bible directed answers wherein is the knowledge needed to avert disaster in all areas of our lives, **[Hosea 4: 6],** considering the "possibility" that the Bible might just be correct in all its presentations?

Where does this gross stupidity come from, that without any reason for doing so, promptly denies the existence of God and rejects his counsel of wisdom? What benefit do these despisers of the goodness of God that leads to repentance, redemption, reconciliation with God and his glory get from their position of rebellion against this God that gave his Son for their temporal and eternal well being, **[John 3: 16]**? There is no profit for soul, mind, body, or spirit, in this profound ignorance, **[Isaiah 5: 13], "Therefore my people are gone into captivity, because they have no knowledge: and their honourable [mighty] men are famished, and their multitude dried up with thirst"**. **[Amos 8: 11]; "Behold, the days come, saith the Lord God, that I will send a famine in the land, not a famine of bread, nor thirst for water, but of hearing the words of the Lord"**.

Is man really so set in his ways of pride, arrogance, ignorance, and stupidity that he won't even explore the possibility that God's Word is true in it's declarations, and prepare accordingly, saving himself an eternity of anguish? Sooner or later, in one way or another, better sooner than later, man will realize it would be better, much better, to be set in God's ways than his own destructive mindset; this mindset of course being where his dilemma's and self destruction comes from. There are many scriptures that speak directly to this; **[Isaiah 5: 20-21], "Woe unto them that call evil good, and good evil; that put darkness for light, and light for darkness; that put bitter for sweet and sweet for bitter! Woe unto them that are wise in their own eyes, and prudent in their own sight"**, *those that are set in their own ways and not God's ways!*

Woe; what an interesting little word. From Webster's Dictionary: and I quote: **Woe: a condition of deep suffering from misfortune, affliction, or grief, calamity, misfortune, sorrow!** *Do you really want this? Your destiny is in your hands.* Take a good look at **[Deuteronomy 30: 19]**; God has given you a choice, told you which way to choose, and given you great incentive for making that choice. What is humanities problem? Can't they follow simple to understand directions for their own good and prosperity? It seems not! Indeed, **What fools ye mortals be!**

Doesn't it seem a bit strange that this man, this created in the likeness of God, a creature that considers himself as being intelligent, would actually choose such idiocy and destruction for himself and his descendents? Just accepting the idea of some unknowledgeable crackpot saying that I evolved from a blob of slime; proceeding through a monkeyism to humanism is certainly not enough for me to accept when my personal eternal future as well as my temporary time "dwelling in this house of clay" is involved. Nor does the acceptance of this by a multitude of blind crackpots following the lead blind crackpot carry any weight either. If my eternal future is going to be based on a theory, it will have to be a theory formed by intelligence much greater and higher than man has exhibited.

Just to consider my present and eternal futures being dependent on human intelligence, including my own, is a scary thought which breeds hopelessness and despair. All this only proves that there is a multitude of blind crackpots among us, which is very apparent from the present condition of the world: crackpots of many varieties that have so adversely affected our world and nation. They are to be found at all levels, positions, and situations of humanity, and they come in all sizes, shapes, and colors applicable to mankind, and certainly in both sexes.

But let's face it; we've also experienced some crackpots who have professed to be Christians. At least they are in a position of exposure to the Bible for correction, unless they are convinced they don't need correction and already know it all. There are some out there like that, sad to say. But regardless of ideas, concepts, perceptions, etc., the questions still need to be answered; the who, what, and why's, that we are all faced with in life that contribute to the knowledge **[Hosea 4:6]** that people need to prevent destruction of themselves and their children. **"My people are destroyed for lack of knowledge: because thou hast rejected knowledge, I will also reject thee that thou shalt be no priest to me: seeing thou hast forgotten the law [WORD] of thy God, I will also forget thy children".**

It is easy to get disgusted and a bit troubled with the contrary conditions, and people, that consistently present their ugly concepts and practices of animosity around us. It seems our national civil "leaders" do nothing to correct the situations, nor can they with their present anti-God mentalities which contribute to the problems, but, **[2 Corinthians 10:4-5], "the weapons of our warfare are not carnal, but mighty through God to the pulling down, destruction, of strongholds; Casting down imaginations, and every high, and low and in between, thing that exalts itself against the knowledge of God, and bringing into captivity every thought to the obedience of Christ".**

It is essential that we be extremely familiar with, and proficient in, the use of these weapons; a sound Biblically renewed mind able and willing to reason according to God's directives, being an essential weapon to start with. It is absolutely imperative that we preserve, maintain, and advance this "knowledge of God" that is so essential to our spiritual growth, development, and correct influence within the sphere of our calling, whether it be in the body of Christ or in the world.

Without this knowledge through obedience to the gospel of God through Jesus and the teaching of the Holy Spirit, we don't have a clue concerning the knowledge of what to be obedient to, nor how to develop and enter into a relationship of fellowship and intimacy with God the Father. This is "what" we were created for; his pleasure, honour, and glory. Our rewards for embracing and adhering to this are beyond our imaginations. **[Hebrews 11:6]** **"But without faith, it is impossible to please him: for he that cometh to God must believe that he is, and that he is a rewarder of them that "diligently" seek him".** Don't mess up your opportunity to walk and talk in fellowship with God. Abide in his presence and he will abide in you, **[John 15:1-15].**

Knowledge of the Unholy

There is another area of knowledge that is of importance for us to acquire in order to know what our "warfare" is all about. This knowledge is also given to us throughout God's Word whereby we may profit. **[2 Timothy 3: 16-17]**, **"ALL scripture is given by inspiration of God, and is profitable for doctrine, for reproof, for correction, for instruction in righteousness: that the man of God may be perfect, thoroughly furnished unto all good works".**

It is wise to know who our enemy is, what his intentions are, and get thorough knowledge on how he operates, and recognize his presence in conditions around us. To not be well aware of him and his tactics is to be ignorant of his devices, thus giving him advantage, **[2 Corinthians 2: 11]**, **"Lest Satan should get an *advantage* of us: for we are not [to be] ignorant of his *devices*"** and, **[Ephesians 4: 27]**, **"Neither give *place* to the devil",** place; being contrary to scriptural teachings. If you take a good, honest look at our world and our own national conditions; you who are educated in this area, at least to some degree, will see that the enemy is quite solidly entrenched all around and among us. This is because of ignorance and being stupid enough to remain ignorant, without knowledge, **[Hosea 4:6].** He even has a strong foothold in some of the denominations of the land and people not recognizing it have accepted it through deception, which is one of his main weapons, and they have perverted Biblical truths to permit these abominations. Indeed **[Isaiah 5: 20] with it's Woe's comes into focus once again.**

One of the most deceptive areas and examples of this is found in **[Matthew 4: 8-9]** and is manifested in a perverted rendition of our Constitution, concerning the erroneously imposed "Separation of Church and State". Under this, our government, along with other anti-God factions, having fallen down in worship to this devil, have created license to declare war on God and excommunicate him and his eternal truths and principles which were designed to give us life. This enemy with his deception is spoken of throughout the Bible for our awareness, education and knowledge, which is essential to our victorious living as being **"more than conquerors through him, JESUS, that loved us", [Romans 8:37].** This enemy is spoken of as Lucifer, Satan, the devil, the evil one, deceiver, accuser of the brethren, destroyer, thief, killer, liar, etc., etc,.

At this point it would be accurate to say anyone in their right mind would not be associated with this enemy of God and humanity in any way. This doesn't leave many in this world, including America, in their right minds, or at least in the minds God created them with and intended for them to enrich and manifest. Due to lack of man's cooperation, things have not gone as well as God intended, but there are exceptions for which I am very thankful, however, we are admonished in **[1 Peter 5:8]** to, **"Be sober, be vigilant; for your adversary the devil, as a roaring lion, walketh about seeking whom he may devour".** The multitudes without Christ are already devoured, it is the exceptions, the redeemed community of Christ; that he is after.

This is but a short introduction to an area of knowledge that has been badly neglected by the vast majority of humanity, resulting in their demise and destruction and being devoured.

I've heard it said by those whose intelligence I have since come to question, that you don't talk about the devil; that just gives him glory. It also keeps us ignorant, and, being ignorant of his devices, **[2 Corinthians 2:11]**, is to not have the knowledge that is necessary to be aware of his presence and working and makes it difficult to make specific preparations for warfare. Being and remaining ignorant of his devices gives him advantage and glory, **[Ephesians 4:27]**. Study these and the adjacent scriptures carefully and see if you have been negligent in any of these areas that need correction concerning the "Resurrection of Excellency".

Let's continue on with "who" we are that also combines with "what" we are. We will always be "who" we are by identification of name, but "what" we are, is determined by our content of heart, our conversation and conduct, the "fruit" that is characteristic of the kind of tree that we manifest by our lifestyle, **[Matthew 7: 15-21]**. Do we have a name that is associated with honor because we maintain a **"tree of life"** lifestyle that produces those things that are commensurate with willing, loving, obedience to the word of God, **"the fruit of the spirit"**, **[Galatians 5:22-23]**?

Please understand, our identification is based on God's determination and opinion of who and what we are, not this world's with all it's anti-God, anti-Bible animosity and total ignorance of what it means to be a Christian. All the noise and clamor they make in opposition to Christianity and Bible principles has been described by our old friend William Shakespeare as **"a tale told by an idiot, full of sound and fury, and signifying nothing"**.

These things of Biblical origin are identified as "good fruit" produced by "good trees" versus evil fruit produced by "corrupt trees". Identification continues on in **[Ephesians 2:10]**, "For we are his workmanship, created in Christ Jesus unto "good works", which God hath before ordained that we should walk in them". These "good works" are further identified in **[1 Corinthians 3: 12-13]** as works of "silver, gold, and precious stones", works when tried by the fire of trials, persecutions, hardships, etc., will not be burned up, but will become more pure.

All these "good things" can be put into one category of **[Acts 10:35], "the reverencing of God and working righteousness, thus being accepted with him".** This is also stated in **[Matthew 7:21]** as **"he that doeth the will of the Father which is in heaven".** There are many other scriptures where this is spoken of, such as **[Psalms 8: 4-6],** and alluded to which the individual is encouraged to "diligently" search out and study for personal growth and development in this **"new and living way" of the gospel of Jesus Christ, [Hebrews 10:20].**

This is a whole new world the majority of humanity knows nothing about, including those who live in the good ole U.S. of A. In spite of the fact we have a large number of churches where delivering the gospel of Jesus Christ, the Bible is found, and to some extent taught, sin still abounds on every hand. It is even to be found in the practices of some, thank God not all, of those very institutions that were established originally as a bulwark against some of the very garbage they now approve of and promote.

It seems that the word of God with its absolutes is not taken very seriously in some of these churches and institutions of higher education, or has just been neglected so long it's been forgotten. It seems these Biblical correctness truths and absolutes have been cast aside in favor of politically correctness, where there no longer seems to be any truth or absolutes of a Biblical nature, having been replaced with acceptance and tolerance of the "if it feels good, do it" culture that has become so popular in our once great nation.

The danger and result of this "forgetting" is warned against in **[Hosea 4:6]**, in the last part of that verse, **"seeing thou hast forgotten the law, word, of thy God, I will also forget thy children". [1Peter 4:17-18], "For the time is come that judgment must begin at the house of God: and if it first begin at us, what shall the end be of them that obey not he gospel of God? And if the righteous scarcely be saved, where shall the ungodly and the sinner appear"?**

Once again the absolute necessity of the **"resurrection of excellency"** arises, but still goes unheeded by the multitudes and sin continues on its relentless destructive march, embraced, practiced, and defended, even in some churches. After all, **we've got our rights, don't we?**

The reality is that the demand and practice of many of these "rights", for the sake of "tolerance" and "diversity" or any other conjured up, deceptive, excuse are not a part of God's agenda that he has set forth for the advancement and well being of his creation. Too late, humanity is going to be made to realize that God has his "rights" too, which supersede ours, and are expressed in his written agenda for all to study and become acquainted with. This would be in pursuit of additional wisdom, following the **"beginning of wisdom" [Psalms 111: 10; Proverbs 9: 10].**

We can see in **[Revelation 21:23-27]**, esp. vs. 27, a vivid example of God's agenda of righteousness and his attitude toward sin and iniquity which we would do well to adopt and emulate. I see no example of diversity or tolerance here, only the inclusion of **"they which are written in the Lamb's book of life.**

It would be good if we could hear more emphasis about God's rights; his right to be loved, honored, revered, worshipped, willingly served with the whole heart, diligently sought and obeyed, etc, etc. Maybe it's becoming apparent, at least to the thinking, inquisitive, person, "why" these of, **[Job 4:19-20], "who dwell in houses of clay are destroyed from morning to evening and perish forever without any regarding it".** There is no "regarding", there is no questioning of the reasons "why" this is taking place so continually, "forever".

In **[Jeremiah 12:11] we have another account of the problems and results spelled out for us, "Many pastors "civil rulers", among others who have attained to various positions of some sort of leadership, have destroyed my vineyard, they have trodden my portion under foot, they have made my pleasant portion a desolate wilderness. They have made it desolate, and being desolate it mourneth unto me; the whole land is made desolate, because no man** *layeth it to heart*"**.** What a picture of America ; **[Amos 8:11]!**

The term *"layeth it to heart"* here is the same as *"regard"* in **[Job 4:20].** The same idea is expressed in pondering, meditating, asking questions about, or simply thinking about these things to ferret out and employ the remedy for them. "Why" do men insist on exercising such stupidity as to destroy themselves when the alternative to such ignorance and destruction is so available and encouraged by God himself for man to take advantage of?

So we live in a democracy, so what. Under this "democracy", sin and abomination of every kind imaginable flourishes and increases, it seems daily; as unborn babies are slaughtered by the millions. And America's abomination of illicit, by God's standards, sexual practices, and perversions, continue to produce and enlarge this disgusting filth. Abortion may be the politically correct name for it, but I prefer to call it like it is. I'm sure that God would agree.

Sexual predators are on the increase with their atrocious practices, spurred on and encouraged by the "legal" sexual arousing pornography industry and their "rights". The drug trade is destroying lives by the score along with some other legal pursuits and industries. Abuse of every kind is occurring constantly throughout our nation and society, and I have only mentioned the very small tip of the iceberg. **[Genesis 6:5], "And God saw that the wickedness of man was great in the earth and that every imagination of the thoughts of his heart was only evil continually"**, and democracy has not provided a solution to this dilemma, nor can it.

When we as a nation do not have the courage nor intelligence to avail ourselves of the God given solution to this atrocious sinful condition that is destroying us, how in heavens name can we, as a nation in such bondage and slavery to sin claim to be **"the land of the free and the home of the brave"**? We are not free because we lack the Biblical imperatives, including intelligence and courage, to correct the sinful dilemmas and abominations of our nation that have insidiously enslaved us, and without the wherewithal to free ourselves, we will very likely remain "enslaved" by our own stupidity.

Thank God for the "few" exceptions among us. The only thing that has changed is that it has gotten worse over the centuries because there are more people. **[Hosea 4:7], "As they increased, so they sinned against me: therefore will I change their glory into *shame*"**. From the condition of our nation it looks like God is keeping his promise. From the looks of the world, it seems that his promise is being witnessed worldwide. Certainly the **"glory of man" [Psalms 8: 5]**, is rapidly turning into shame and he has no one to blame but himself. Man has become so accustomed to this wretchedness that it has become the norm for his existence and he doesn't even realize that he is in deep, deep, trouble; talk about the blind leading the blind!

Once again I must call to mind **[Hosea 4:6], "My people are destroyed for lack of knowledge".** When you are not even smart enough to realize you are being destroyed while it is in progress, and promoting and enjoying much of it, you have to admit, that's the height of stupidity. Even a dumb bug, if he senses he is in danger will scurry for cover: but not man, he creates his own destruction, revels in it, and claims to be free. Little did Shakespeare realize the enormity of his statement, **"What fools ye mortals be".** Again, **[Job 4:20-21], "They are destroyed from morning to evening: they perish forever without any regarding it".**

It may come as a big shock to some people, but democracy is not the answer God has provided for man to deliver him from his wretchedness of abominations. There is no repentance of sin or forgiveness in democracy. It's just another form of human government; whether it is the best or not depends entirely on who's at the helm; who's in control, who's running it. What are its principles and policies, its goals; who or what is setting the standards for these? Are they standards of excellence that will encourage and lead the people that a government is meant to serve and lead to higher standards of excellence that promotes the highest good and well-being as outlined by God in his Word of Truth and life?

Are the leaders in this government of a quality and character who can and will do this? What about majority rule; are the majority of a mind that will prevent the destruction of the whole, or are they a selfish lot comprised of "self interest groups", that insist on having their way with an "if it feels good, do it" mentality regardless of the fact that past experience has proven their will to be disastrous to the nation as a whole?

If an individual person or nation is in a condition that demands change for the enrichment of quality of its life, *there must first, as a necessity, be a significant upgrading in the thinking and thought processes.* **[Isaiah 55:7-9], "Let the wicked forsake his way, and the unrighteous man his thoughts; and let him return to the Lord, and he will have mercy upon him; and to our God, for he will abundantly pardon. For my thoughts are not your thoughts, neither are your ways my ways, saith the Lord. For as the heavens are higher than the earth, so are my ways higher than your ways, and my thoughts than your thoughts".**

This demands change to begin at the "higher" levels of government, both church and state in cooperation with God, and every other area of leadership, including parenting, in order to lead and teach those who are following and expected to follow who themselves, all to soon, will have to take over the reins of leadership.

Blind leadership will not only lead the blind but will cause ever increasing and extensive blindness in those who willingly and foolishly follow. Thank God there are exceptions to this; there are those who recognize the blindness and error ahead, see the ditch of destruction the others fail to see, and refuse to follow the corrupt leadership, but choose to walk in this **"new and living way"** and to **"study to show themselves approved unto God".**

We have some examples of these individuals found throughout the Bible, who because of their commitment to God and his word, prevailed in the most demanding and trying circumstances. Joseph was one of the better known ones. Accounts of four of the more famous Biblical characters are found in the book of Daniel including their exploits. Apparently these young men were not of the contrary, disobedient, lifestyle that caused the Israelites to be taken into captivity, but because they were of that nation and people, they were taken along with the others. However, because of their devotion and commitment to serve God rather than man, God caused them to excel and be victorious even in their captivity.

Even among the general populace of the people who are destroyed because they have rejected knowledge, there can be those exceptions who because of their personal commitment to, and relationship with God, are excepted from the destruction. At other times they will be singled out for destruction because of the stand they take. Either way, it is in God's hands. **[Matthew 10:28] "And fear not them which kill the body, but are not able to kill the soul: but rather fear him which is able to destroy both body and soul in hell".** It is a good thing this relationship with God is on a personal basis and not dependent on others. Only through Jesus Christ can this relationship be established, by **"repentance from sin and believing the gospel unto obedience", [Mark 1: 15].** See **[2 Chronicles 7: 14]** for the four ingredients of repentance.

Obedience: now there's an interesting subject worthy of intense consideration, **obedience to the gospel of God, his teachings unto righteousness, holiness, Godliness, the Fruit of the Spirit, etc.** Is it possible that lack of knowledge, ignorance of, and refusal of obedience [doing] of these things that please God were, and are, the cause of people being destroyed continually? **The [John 8: 29] "doing always those** "things" that please him" and the employment of [Hebrews 6: 9] "better things that accompany salvation" have always been and continue to be his requirements, and the rejection of these "things" still leads to destruction, [Romans 6;23].

What these "things" are is another whole area of in-depth personal study that in itself is certainly an integral part of the "excellency" that was originally created in us whereby we may profit in all ways for always. Just the identifying and listing of these "things" is an essential, worthwhile endeavor that will lead into intense study and Biblical enlightenment. Try it, you'll like it; it might even become a major part of your lifestyle. That would be a pleasant change for the bulk of humanity, mostly among those who at the present time are vehemently expressing their erroneous opposition to it.

Sin always has, still does, and always will carry its own retribution. Sin is still sin, and the wages of sin is still death, and political correctness and democracy has not and cannot change that fact nor provide a remedy for it. God has not and will not change his agenda, just because some people choose to disagree with him and or disbelieve and reject him, regardless of how important they seem to think they are. Disagree with me if you are so inclined, it means nothing; disagreeing with God, however, bears eternal consequences.

There are no exceptions to this. God's word is immutable and absolute. Live by accepting, embracing, and doing it; or die by rejecting, neglecting, and despising it, the choice is yours. **[2 Peter 3: 9] ---"The Lord is not willing that any should perish, but that all should come to repentance".** This includes you. **[John 3: 16-17] "For God so loved the world that he gave his only begotten Son, that whosoever believeth on him should not perish, but have everlasting life. For God sent not his Son into the world to condemn the world; but**

that the world through him might be saved". You, I, we, all, are a part of this world that Jesus died for so that we might live; don't mess it up.

We have dealt a little bit with "who" this man creature is, and "what" he is. We have gone into the reasons "why" he "is destroyed for lack of knowledge". Certainly more could be said about these things as we study more and allow the Holy Spirit the time we need to give him to teach us in-depth about these things. We all seem to have something in common; we learn slowly about the things above and we learn with difficulty. I can only surmise that it is because of the sinful nature we were born with that has a large degree of pride that resists being corrected, even when we know correction is needed.

Christians are no exception to this. We are expected to correct our children as needed for proper development, why shouldn't God correct us for the same reason? Just because you are of adult age and don't think you need God's correction any more, you are the most stupid among all the stupid, **[Proverbs 1: 7], "The fear of the Lord is the beginning of knowledge: *but fools despise wisdom and instruction*".** The medicine of humility is quite often hard to swallow. I've choked on it a few times myself. However in **[1 Peter 5:5-6] we are admonished; "Yea, all of you be subject one to another, and be clothed with humility; for God resisteth the proud, and giveth grace to the humble. Humble YOURSELVES therefore under the mighty hand of God, that he may exalt you in due time".**

Let's face it, in the areas of personal spiritual development, advancement, and enrichment, man has proven himself to have nothing to be proud of. There is also much to be realized and considered with this that comes to light with additional study, **[2 Timothy 2:15]** and meditation, **[Psalms 1:2]** before God. This is all a part of **[1 Timothy 4:7] "exercising ourselves in**

Godliness" on our journey of growing and developing in **"The Resurrection of Excellency"** that God originally created in us. It is not a difficult journey once you get a **"vision of the value"** of the rewards along the way as outlined in God's word.

There is no doubt that this is one of the main reasons mankind doesn't pursue and, **[Colossians 3:2] "set his affection on things above, and not on things on the earth".** He has not fixed his mind and heart on the **[Romans 2: 4] "riches of God's goodness, forbearance, and longsuffering; not knowing that the goodness of God leads him to repentance".**

And he knows nothing about this **"excellency of God"** that lies dormant within him, waiting to be discovered and resurrected unto its rightful position of dominion power, forcing the sinful nature into subjection and dormancy and eventual annihilation. Another reason for this neglect is found in **[Ecclesiastes 12: 12, "much study is a weariness to the flesh".** That means hard work, and man doesn't like hard work, even when the benefits are beyond his comprehension. Man has become extremely lazy, especially where pursuit of righteousness and holiness are concerned.

Many Christians have lived powerless lives because they have been taught that they are "sinners' saved by grace, and so they do what sinners do, sin. After all, they are saved by grace so what's the problem. The problem is they are still bound under the title of "sinner", so there is no challenge to change. They need to be indoctrinated with the realization that there is a place above and beyond it as a "new creature" in Christ saved by grace. **[2 Corinthians 5:17-18] "Therefore IF any man be in Christ, he is a NEW creature: old things, including the title sinner, are passed away; behold, ALL things are become new. And all, these new, things are of God, who**

hath reconciled us to himself by Jesus Christ, and hath given to us the ministry of reconciliation".

This is a place where the things of sin we used to enjoy become abhorrent to us. The things that used to thrill our senses are now detestable and turn our stomachs. We now become very conscious of things that displease God and desire only to please him. Life takes on meaning with purpose, with pleasing God being that purpose, where before it was just something that came and went from day to day, and we were conditioned to follow traditions and customs without question because that's the way life was, and that's what everybody else did.

Grandpa and grandma grew up as sinners saved by grace, Mom and Dad grew up as sinners saved by grace, and I was taught the same thing and grew up the same way. Then I started reading and studying God's word for myself and realized that God never created me to be a sinner, never wanted me to be one, and provided a way to not be one anymore. I read that the **blood of Jesus cleansed me from ALL unrighteousness and that I was cleansed from sin through the,** *applied*, **[John 15: 3] word that God had spoken to us and the Holy Spirit was teaching me.**

Sin became something to be hated as God hates it. It disappoints God, grieves the Holy Spirit; and it hurts and destroys people. To indulge in it when professing to be a Christian was to make null and void the work of the cross, and to even maintain the title of sinner after being washed in the blood was an insult to the power of the blood and the name of Jesus.

If I was to be a Christian, I had to be a *"new creature in Christ"* and accept the challenges of **[Romans 12:2],"renewing my mind"** and **[John 8:29], "doing always**

those things that please God", and "learning, embracing, and doing, [Hebrews 6:9], "those things that accompany salvation", and "growing in the grace and knowledge of our Lord and Saviour Jesus Christ", [2 Peter 3: 18]. It bothered me when well meaning Christians attempted to hang that old filthy cloak of sin back on me, for whatever reason or excuse they had, after the blood of Jesus had removed it. **Bless God; he whom the Son has set free is free indeed, [John 8:36],** free from the bondage of sin with its filth and destruction wherein this world wallows while suffering under a delusion of freedom. The first line of a simple little chorus comes to mind **"Take this whole world but give me Jesus".**

It is rather amazing, how that once you have become a Christian and spent some time gaining knowledge and understanding along with wisdom and accumulated intelligence you can look at the world you used to be a part of and wonder how man is so foolish as to inundate himself with such a complete sense of hopelessness for his future, both temporal and eternal. If, however, your mind and attention is so buried in, and distracted by the "things of this world" and the deceptive momentary pleasures, comforts, and conveniences, it provides, it is easy to understand the spiritual blindness that it causes.

Distractions are problems for all of us, and there are plenty of them. That is why it is so necessary for us to get our minds involved in the admonition of **[Philippians 4: 6-9]**, establishing the importance of Biblical, spiritual values so our activities tend to gravitate to their establishment and promotion. As these "values" develop and accumulate, they become our priorities and pursuits, and the legitimate things of this world that are necessary to every day life will find their own places to fit in and contribute to our necessities. One of these wonderful "values" is not very common in our world of turmoil and strife.

It is not common because the very values themselves that would displace the turmoil and strife have been rejected, neglected, and despised. This particular value is "peace", **[Psalms 119:165], "GREAT PEACE have they that love thy law "word" and [nothing shall offend them]", or [be a stumbling block to them].** Though I am a fan of the KJV, I do prefer the use of the **"stumbling block"** terminology here as found in some of the other versions. It seems to have a more precise guidance as to a character development of self-discipline and control. All sin should be offensive to the Christian, but none of it a stumbling block.

One may be offended at the many adverse things taking place in our nation but still maintain a spiritual composure and stability that will prompt a suitable Biblical response rather than a worldly type reaction, a response that tends to peaceful settlements if at all possible, rather than reactions that tend to violence and revenge. This has nothing to do with "political correctness", but everything to do with "Biblical Correctness", something our "civil leaders" either know nothing about or don't have the courage to introduce from their public pulpits, platforms, or positions to our people and nation.

Our national, worldly dilemma's can only be solved with spiritual input based on "what thus saith the Lord" the Word of God, the Bible. There is no input from other sources including contrary religions regardless of how "politically correct", "tolerant", or "diverse" the malcontents opposed to the Christian faith in our society insist we should be to gain their approval.

The Christian segment of society was never created nor intended to gain the approval of the rebellious, disobedient, sinful element that has turned their backs on God and despise his word. If they want tolerance, let them show tolerance toward the Bible and the truth and absolutes it presents for the total well-being of all, including themselves. If they want diversity, let them diversify toward inclusion of these principles of God's Word for their redemption and reconciliation.

We continue to witness the mass of humanity of whom it is spoken in **[Job 4: 20], "They are destroyed from morning to evening: they perish for ever without any regarding it. Doth not their excellency which is in them go away? They die, even without wisdom"**. "What" is this excellency? We could enter into quite a discussion on this, and I'm sure there would be much constructive input concerning it with much disagreement also. Who knows, we might even learn something in the process of such discussion and input if we will expand the horizons of our thinking and thought processes to include all Gods word without getting hung up on man's traditions and customs, including his pet denominational doctrines.

[Ephesians 4: 14], "That we be henceforth no more children, tossed to and fro, and carried about with every wind of doctrine, by the sleight of men, and cunning craftiness, whereby they lie in wait to deceive". **[Matthew 15:9], "But in vain do they worship me, teaching for doctrines the commandments of men"**.

NOTES

IV. THE EXCELLENCY WITHIN

Man's mind, or his heart, such as it is, the terms are somewhat interchangeable, depending on the situations and circumstances at hand. At times they may be referred to as the "new" or "inner man", thus his thinking, thoughts, and ways, due to his sinful nature, even with God's help and assistance, have a difficult time fixating on the positive, but instead, seems to have an overwhelming propensity for the negative. Keeping our heads straightened out mentally even under the best of intentions becomes somewhat of, a "warfare" at times.

The counsel we find in [2 Corinthians 10: 4-5] is primarily for Christians; **"For the weapons of our warfare are not carnal, but mighty through God to the pulling down of strongholds; Casting down imaginations, and every high thing that exalteth itself against the knowledge of God, and bringing into captivity every thought to the captivity of Christ"**.

This is nevertheless good information for the sinner as well as the saints of God, being, however, a bit beyond the sinner as there are some steps to becoming a saint that need to be initiated prior to getting an understanding of the need for such admonition. Many are the saints that have not yet gotten a good grasp on this essential, for our imaginations, thinking, and thoughts, be they good or evil, determine our next steps in life from our speech to, and including our conduct. This thinking and thoughts would generally be associated with the mind but are spoken as the abundance of the heart, [Matthew 12: 34-35; Luke 6: 45], **"A good man out of the good treasure of his heart bringeth forth that which is good; and an evil man out** of the evil treasure of his heart bringeth forth that which is evil: for of the abundance of the heart his mouth speaketh".

This is good advice for all people, but the non-Christian is not likely to recognize or accept the significance of it. Many professing Christians are guilty of this as well. I am convinced that there is much more to learn about these **weapons of warfare, strongholds,** and the **gates of hell, [Matthew 16:18],** and what they consist of, and how to use the weapons to combat and destroy the strongholds and gates of hell than any of us realize. Unfortunately many Christians, both the ones that are of **"full age"** as well as the **"babes", [Hebrews 5: 12-14],** have trouble from time to time maintaining their spiritual equilibrium when it comes to acquiring and building a spiritually healthy abundance of the mind and heart, and inadvertently erect gates of hell against themselves as well as others. Thus we are given, in an attempt to overcome any evil tendency, scriptures such as, **[Colossians 3:2], "Set, fix, your affection on the things above, not on the things of earth".** This will come about as we, **[2 Timothy 2:15], "Study to show ourselves approved unto God, a workman that needeth not to be ashamed, rightly dividing the word of truth",** thus enabling us to: **[Romans 12:1-2], "I beseech you therefore, brethren, by the mercies of God, that ye present your bodies a living sacrifice to God, which is your reasonable service. And be not conformed to this world: but be ye transformed by the renewing of your mind, that ye may prove what is that good, and acceptable and perfect will of God". [Psalms 119: 11], "Thy word have I hid in my heart that I might not sin against thee".**

This all is contributive to, and lends itself to the awareness of **"their excellency that is in them", [Job 4:21].** This will also raise the awareness of the subtle, devious sinful things that tend to our destruction and the dissipation of this "excellency" and the loss of Godly wisdom which is an essential part of it. This is all contingent on a correct attitude towards God's Word including the value we as individuals place on it. If we don't see enough value in it to **"delight in it and meditate on it, [Psalms 1: 2], love it, [Psalms 119: 165], hide it in our hearts, [Psalms 119: 11], and study it, [2 Timothy 2: 15], then it is time to examine the relationship we claim to have and our love for our Lord.**

It would seem to be a bit negative to even talk about man's sinfulness and the abominations and destruction it causes, but if not brought to the surface and made known, man has no idea of that of which he needs to repent and be delivered from. Even with all the information and knowledge available, in our post modern days of relativity input and deception, there is a cloud of confusion of his own making that has engulfed man concerning good and evil, right versus wrong and how to react or respond properly in any given situation. We do have multitudes of "our own countrymen, fellow Americans" who are not interested in availing themselves of such information and knowledge, but have reduced themselves to an "if it feels good, do it" existence.

This is destructive to themselves, all those in contact with them, beginning with their loved ones, and their nation. It does, however, take a certain amount of intelligence to even be concerned about such things and respond intelligently to this concern. Nevertheless, the negativism of it all is counteracted by the accentuating of the Godly **"excellency that is in them"**, which begins with **"Repent ye and believe the gospel" [Mark 1:15].** This **"excellency that is in them"** needs to be acknowledged, accepted, and taught in order for people to know it is a part of their original design that God intended for them to exercise for his glory and our own well-being.

If we can accept being created in God's image and likeness, there is no reason for us to reject the concept of his "excellency" as a part of his likeness and to realize he originally created it within us. There is no way we, in our limited, finite, minds can even begin to comprehend this majestic God of creation, or understand the extent of his love for us or the abundance of his provision for us and in us. He does give us unlimited things to think about concerning all this and allows us to use our imaginations with discretion while using Godly wisdom as our guide.

There is in **[Ephesians 3:19]** another word that may give us some additional insight into God's provision on our behalf, **"And to know the love of Christ, which passeth knowledge, that ye may be filled with all the FULLNESS of God"**. Now we have his **image, likeness, his excellency, and his "fullness"** to consider as his desire for us to live therein, for indeed **in him is his desire for us to live and move and have our being, our completeness, fulfillment and purpose, [Acts 17:28]**.

He that has a mind to think, let him exercise himself in study, thought, and meditation concerning these things, and surely the God of peace will be with him. We will never in this world understand all these things, but that does not keep us from simply accepting it, pursuing it, and enjoying it, whether we understand it or not.

[2 Peter 1:2-4], "Grace and peace be multiplied unto you through the knowledge of God, and of Jesus Christ our Lord. According as his divine power hath given unto us all things that pertain unto life and godliness, through the knowledge of him that hath called us to glory and virtue: Whereby are given to us exceeding great and precious promises: that by these ye might be partakers of the divine

nature, having escaped the corruption that is in the world through lust".

There are some very interesting things in these verses that feed into the fullness of God. **Vs.2,** *The more our knowledge of God the Father and Jesus our Lord is increased, the more grace and peace is multiplied to us.* **Vs.3,** Once again this **"knowledge" of God becomes an element of his divine power by which he has given us all things that pertain to life and Godliness, Vs. 4.**

Because of all this we now are blessed with **"exceeding great and precious promises that enable us to be partakers of his divine nature", or shall we say "his divine likeness, or divine fullness, or divine excellency.** God has not withheld anything from those who, with enthusiasm, **[Deuteronomy 28:47] "serve him with joyfulness and with gladness of heart for the abundance of all things".** The more we pursue these things, the more our eyes of understanding will be enlightened and knowledge gained.

It is intelligence and wisdom to enter into that pursuit; even just plain common sense demands it given the fact it all continually contributes to our promotion, development, and over all well being in all areas of life. Why would anyone with even a just a beginning of common sense turn their backs on this? The answer is simple; they have been raised in an environment where that common sense is absent. Thus they have not been taught this common sense that borders on the "beginning of wisdom", the fear and reverencing of God, which is discouraged by the "separation of church and state" fallacy. The insertion of this in the constitution, regardless of Jefferson's intention, is nothing but a subtle attempt at a "separation of God and people". As a result, the people are farther removed from the realization and knowledge of his image, likeness, excellency, fullness, divine nature, etc.

And America continues in her demise and decline into the degradation of rebellion against God, led by the anti-God, anti-Christ elements of "our own countrymen" residing within our borders who claim to be Americans, but deny the very Biblical principles upon which America is founded and became America. **"And their excellency which is in them" remains unknown, unrevealed, unacknowledged, and undeveloped: it goes away, and they die, even without wisdom", [Job 4: 21].**

It is because of pseudo authority in leadership positions with its erroneous, counter-productive influences, that these willingly deceived leaders drag multitudes of others down with them. Once again we see the, *"blind leading the blind"*, principle in graphic display. When are the blind followers going to wake up and start using their own minds for beneficial, God honoring uses and results for themselves and others around them including their own future posterity? If the blind leaders insist on going into the ditch of destruction, let them go by themselves.

By their own waywardness, disobedience, and rebellion, they disqualify themselves as leaders and deserve no ones support and allegiance. **[Luke 12: 48], "For unto whom much is given, of him shall be much required: and to whom men have committed much, of him they will ask the more"**. Servants may well serve at the pleasure and discretion of the leaders whatever their capacity and position may be: **[Matthew 23: 11], "But he that is greatest among you shall be your servant"**. Be that as it may be, wisdom and intelligence will demand, even of servants, to use discretion about who they serve. A servant at his best cannot be of service if his service for the purpose of well being to all is sidetracked by service to a blind leader who will destroy all who follow him.

Leaders and servants must realize that they serve together at the pleasure and discretion of Almighty God and his counsel of righteousness, His Word. Whoever violates this sacred trust, immediately and without ceremony, forfeits their position, authority, and anointing with which they began their tenure. **[Psalms 133: 1], "Behold, how good and how pleasant it is for brethren to dwell together in unity". [I Corinthians 1: 10], "Now I beseech you, brethren, by the name of our Lord Jesus Christ, that ye all speak the same thing , and that there be no divisions among you; but that ye be** *perfectly joined together in the* <u>*same mind*</u> *and in* <u>*the same judgment*</u>*"*.

This is only possible and can take place if we do indeed, **"have the mind of Christ", [1 Corinthians 2: 16].** Read and study **[John 17], the Lords prayer,** to get a clear idea of how essential unity is to the success of the family of God, the Body of Christ and God's regard for it. Unity for God's pleasure, honour, and glory always trumps any concepts that we may develop along the way that are contrary and damaging to this unity.

There are qualifications found in God's Word for leaders, and first of all they must be Godly men wherein the likeness and excellency of God is apparent and evident. Some of our founding fathers lacked these qualifications but were at least conscious of and sympathetic toward the need of Biblical principles as the anchor and foundation for the new nation they were responsible for forming and setting in place. They gave us, however, a constitution that DID NOT INCLUDE a separation of church and state perversion in it. That came later under the direction of men of much lesser quality and character.

We can find the likeness of this situation in **[Judges 2: 10]**, **"And also all that generation were gathered unto their fathers: and there arose another generation after them, which knew not the Lord, nor the works that he had done for [America]**. Pardon the substitution of America for Israel. It fits either way, or you may use them both.

Any way you look at it, America is suffering under the curse of **[Hosea 4:6], "My people are destroyed for lack of knowledge: because thou has rejected knowledge [of God], I will reject thee that thou shalt be no priest to me: because thou hast forgotten [and cast away] the law [word] of thy God, I will also forget thy children"**.

This whole scenario of idiocy is a result of rejecting the direction of God in **[Deuteronomy 30: 19], and choosing death and cursing rather than life and blessing.** This was done after God specifically told them that their children would only live if they themselves would choose life and blessing; God's Word of truth and absolutes, rather than deception and disobedience; righteousness and holiness, rather than sin and iniquity! What a classic example of man's stupidity and foolishness.

[Psalms 111:10; Proverbs 1:7; 5: 12; 9:10] In these scriptures we find that **"the fear of the Lord is the beginning of wisdom and knowledge"** with the addition of **understanding** to round out the requirements for a productive, profitable lifestyle, acceptable unto the Lord. We also find that fools despise wisdom, instruction, and reproof. They have no understanding or knowledge, and have become such profound fools that they don't even understand that their whole lifestyle is steeped in foolishness that they have been deceived into believing is the truth. The great deceiver and father of lies is very good at his abominable profession of deception.

[Acts 10:35] gives us **"the working of righteousness"** along with **"fearing God"** as a basic requirement for being accepted with God. Allow me to add a couple of others that are close companions that are as scarce as the basic requirements themselves. They are intelligence and common sense, the exercise of which may be included in the **"working of righteousness"**. The question now arises; if the fear of the Lord is just the beginning of these things, what is needed to attain to a greater accumulation and operation of these necessities?

I really have to conclude that humanity is not very intelligent; as a matter of fact, rather stupid. When God made life and blessing with his excellency available to them and told them which one to choose, and why; they still, even to this day, choose to remain in a state of death and cursing with its hopelessness, despair, and destruction for themselves and their children is testimony to their stupidity. Well has Shakespeare said; **"What fools ye mortals be"**. As God has blessed America so abundantly, so may he now equally have mercy on us as we learn to bless Him as He has blessed us, initiating **[2 Chronicles 7: 14]**.

I never cease to marvel at the fact that with the mental abilities man has retained and developed, even in his sinful state, the knowledge he has attained to through his learning processes, etc. With that attainment, he still, generally, has not arrived at the "beginning of wisdom" and the intelligence to **[Deuteronomy. 30:19]**, **"choose life rather than death",** and continues to rebel against the giver and author of life, **Almighty God.**

Man continues to prove this fact by his never ending wretchedness, displayed on the world scene hour after hour and day after day. **[Genesis 6: 5]**, **"And God saw that the** wickedness of man was great in the earth and that every imagination of his heart was only evil continually". [Job 4: 20-21], "They are destroyed from morning to evening: they perish for ever without any regarding it. Doth not their *excellency which is in them* go away? They die, even without wisdom". [Hosea 4:7], "As they were increased, so they sinned against me: therefore I will change their glory into shame".

America may well still be the greatest nation on earth, but she is in a very shameful state of being for she has failed continually to bless God with love, obedience, and gratitude for the never ending abundances of blessings God has given her. [John 3: 16], "For God so loved the world, that he gave his only begotten Son, that whosoever believeth on him should not perish but have everlasting life".

Instead of the **"God Bless America"** we hear quite often, and He has done this with great abundance, it is well past time for American's and America to **"gird up the loins of their minds," [1 Peter 1: 13],** and bless God in return with profound love, obedience, and devotion, in gratitude for his past and present abundance, provision, and blessings.

Whether or not these blessings continue or we see an increase in the curses we are bringing on ourselves through rejection of God, His truth and absolutes, is entirely up to us and whether or not we correct the erroneous choices we have made and continue to make. America has not done well in this area, and **"the excellency which is in them continues to dissipate and go away, and they continue to die, even without wisdom",** never knowing that this excellency was just a choice away. Indeed Mr. Shakespeare, **"What fools ye mortals be."**

NOTES

NOTES

V. STATE OF THE HEART

There are many scriptures that pertain to the conditioning, or the "State of the Heart." We are instructed in **[Proverbs 4: 23],"Keep thy heart with all diligence; for out of it are the issues of life."** It would seem that the need for "diligence" is emphasized here simply by use of the word itself. No half hearted attempt at developing and maintaining of character and abundance of heart is acceptable as it will always be insufficient to the need, and will invariably fall short of the requirements needed for **"the abundance of the heart"** to issue forth life rather than death.

Of such is the nature of man unless there is something exterior to his natural inclination of sinfulness that is able to correct and direct his life's journey. Several scriptures in The Psalms point to the relationship with God as involving the **"whole heart"** in various ways. I would encourage the readers to search these scriptures out for in-depth study for accumulation of knowledge that can be passed on to others for the benefit of all. Therein do we find the admonition to **"hide God's word in our heart so that we might not sin against him", [Psalms 119: 11].**

Now we have to bring the mind into consideration as the heart and mind are quite often linked together and may mean the same thing as all inclusive of the new man. We find this in **[Romans 12: 2]** where the heart is not mentioned but the necessity of a "diligently" kept, prepared, and "renewed" mind to Biblical standards and values is of the utmost importance. **"Be not conformed to this world, but be ye transformed by the "diligent" and continual renewing of your mind, that ye may prove what is that good, and acceptable, and perfect** will of God." This will only be accomplished by a determined **"Study to show thyself approved unto God, a workman that needeth not to be ashamed, rightly dividing the word of truth", [2Timothy 2:15].** It would seem that if there is going to be a proving in our lives of what is that good, and acceptable, and perfect will of God that can only take place through the avenue of a **"diligently kept heart and renewed mind."**

This is all based on the input of God's word of truth and absolutes for daily counsel and guidance that has been **"hid and stored in the heart, and becomes the "abundance of the heart" [Luke 6: 45].** You may well be a recipient of God's amazing grace, but if you neglect the requirements that produce a renewed mind and diligently kept heart, you will lead a defeated, problematic life, even as a professing Christian. The evil output of an evil heart mentioned in this scripture emphasizes the need for the heart and mind to be in the constant care and nurturing of, **abiding in,** God's Word. **[John 15:7], "If ye abide in me, and my words abide in you, ye shall ask what ye will, and it shall be done unto you".**

At this point even though you may think you know what it means to **"abide"**, let me encourage you to dig out your dictionary and take a quick refresher course on it to get a better understanding of what it is to "abide". To abide or not to abide; that is the question: this, of course is based on our own choice and knowledge of the word. Let me insert my own definition of abide: to take up, establish residence; this I believe will be supported by a dictionary definition.

"Therefore choose life that both thou and thy seed; descendents, children, may live", [Deuteronomy 30:19]. There is one of two things which may work together simultaneously that are needed here for this choice to be made. First, there is the *intelligence* to perceive the **"goodness of**

God" [Romans 2: 4], and choose it for its own value and sake, the resultant benefits and rewards, or second, the *desperation* to escape the sinful existence and problems that accompany it, and are characteristic of a sin orientated existence.

Several years ago there was a catchy little phrase that was used quite extensively by many who wished to show some semblance of brilliance and glean some admiration and esteem from others by the use thereof. That phrase was **"state of the art"**, which as I understand, was meant to convey a thought of extreme quality to the object being referred to. It was quite an impressive little quote and sounded equally impressive to the benefit of those who used it, and I suppose many of those who heard it being used.

Although it never made much sense, at least it sounded good and seemed to convey the thought as was intended. The president would give his state [condition] of the union, or nation, address, a pastor his state of the church address, or others their state of whatever they were speaking of address. If it was a large corporation, such as Enron, the state, or condition maybe was not as it was presented to be, and consequently people suffered great loss. But such is the result of deception for whatever purpose the deceiver has in mind. But like all fads, it seemed to have run its course, lost its punch and prestige, and is seldom heard anymore.

However, regardless of the state, or condition of what was being referred to, it seems to be the nature of man to be a little bit fraudulent in his presentation of that state, especially if there were hidden agendas and discrepancies afoot; which if they were planned discrepancies, reveals the deceptive **"state of the heart"**, or possibly "hearts", of those in control of such events. It is this condition, the "state, or abundance, of the heart" whither good or evil, that I wish to call attention to in this writing. This as a condition that the Bible addresses from cover to cover, a condition we all have to deal with on a moment by moment, daily basis that produces temporal benefits that must be properly viewed and experienced to be appreciated as well as eternal benefits and rewards promised, but yet to be enjoyed.

The basic difference between the Biblical "state of the heart" versus a non-biblical condition is found in several scriptures, a notable one in **[Deuteronomy 30: 19],** mentioned previously. The Biblical state is rewarded with life and blessing, whereas the non-biblical condition, abundance, or "state" of evil and abomination is cursed with death and additional cursing. I make no claim to being the smartest person in the world, but even I can figure out that life and blessing with their overall, God promised benefits are much to be preferred to death and cursing with its resultant temporal and eternal penalties and horrors.

The majority of stuff this catchy little ditty was applied to was just that, "stuff", of material content, the value of which seldom, with exceptions, lasted as long as the ditty did and was seldom as impressive as the ditty sounded. There are other things that have come on the scene of humanity that I would have to regard as truly "state of the art" quality. There are things that have come, remained, and blessed mankind; some in their existence, but others in their usage as their existence continues.

Even the existence of the Bible, with its value, which will always remain, becomes negligible in its benefits if it is not put to its intended use. Writings of glorious nature, that have come at the inspiration of divine guidance that have touched the hearts and minds of concerned individuals, have truly brought life and life more abundantly to those who "gladly received" such words. These words of instruction and knowledge are at the height, and above man perceived, the "state of the art" quality, as they are instrumental in securing the God required "State of the Heart" that is essential for this life and life more abundantly.

Man has settled for a multitude of stuff that has been considered as "state of the art", that has robbed him of more than it could possibly contribute to his good and wellbeing; stuff that was never designed for his benefit, but only for gratification of his feelings and emotions and make the producers thereof wealthy.

There are other things that must be considered such as the art of paintings that have commended themselves to the list of notables, and some music compositions that provide stirrings to the soul and revitalization to the spirit that have remained of great aesthetic and spiritual value to humanity long after the composers of such paintings and music have passed on.

There is much to be considered here as to the "state of the heart" of these various artists with their contributions to mankind along with what inspired and compelled them to produce such stirring items. Regardless, somewhere along the way we must realize that such contributions of the various talents could not be accomplished without God's contribution of his likeness and excellence within us that enabled such conditions, items, and events. There are people who would seem to be handicapped who do some rather astounding things, such as playing a piano, plus other amazing things that we with, seemingly all our faculties, struggle with.

Where did such talent come from when not learned by conventional means? Why do some people have natural abilities to do certain things and excel at them while others do not? Some people can do by natural abilities what others have to learn, sometimes with great difficulty, from "scratch", and even then never seem to arrive to where the "naturalists" excelled with a minimum of effort.

Much is to be learned and acknowledged of God's greatness and majesty with which he has so generously and abundantly blessed humanity. And all he asks of us is to honor him with obedience to his divine principles, **[Matthew 22: 37-40], "Jesus said unto him, Thou shalt love the Lord thy God with all thy heart, and with all thy soul, and with all thy mind. This is the first and great commandment. And the second is like unto it, Thou shalt love thy neighbor as thyself. On these two commandments hang all the law and the prophets."**

If man would exercise himself to know, understand, and meet the demands of this "love", what a different world we would have today. Regardless of the abundance of grace, there are certain conditions and demands that are necessary for meeting the requirements of this love. These things are all basically contained in being willingly "obedient".

There is an abundance of knowledge man needs to attain to, **[Hosea 4:6], as requirements for life, living, health, and happiness;** and at the head of this list of requirements would have to be, of course, THE HOLY BIBLE with it's introduction of Jesus Christ, Saviour and King to humanity; God's own Living Word to mankind for his guidance, nurture, prosperity, and profit, which man generally, has to his own demise, rejected, and despised. Well has William Shakespeare said **"What fools ye mortals be"**!

Unfortunately, even in some Christian circles this Word is neglected to the point of creating some "gates of hell" within the body of Christ and erecting some strongholds that are a constant source of irritation, thorns in the flesh, or worse, so to speak. It is a part of God's goodness, **[Romans 2: 4],** that God's grace "is sufficient" for our spiritual maintenance whenever we stumble and fall along the way.

But his counsel and direction is not only sufficient, but absolutely essential for our Spiritual growth and development unto the smashing of these gates of hell and pulling down strongholds unto victory; not settling for mere maintenance while effectively dealing with these oppositions to the gospel. It is and has always been God's intention that we be **[Romans 8:37] "more than conquerors through him that loved, and continues to love, us".**

There is another whole area of knowledge that has been neglected that is essential to avert the destruction spoken of in **[Hosea 4:6].** This is a good working knowledge of the enemy and adversary of our soul, Satan, who comes not but for to steal, kill, and destroy the provision God wants you to have and enjoy today, tomorrow, and forever. There is no other place you can get the necessary information on him but through God's Word, by His divine counsel. It is essential that we have this knowledge in order to recognize his deceit and scheming and stop his evil encroachment and invasion of our lives.

Adam and Eve didn't seem to have this safe guard of knowledge, and not having understanding of the seriousness of their transgression, brought the curse of sin on us all. And we ignorant human beings, in spite of all the horrible examples resulting from this, many of which we can witness on television every hour of the day or night, continue to do the same stupid thing, choosing death and cursing in our daily lives instead of God's provision of life and blessing through Jesus Christ our Lord and Saviour. And the unsaved like to consider themselves as intelligent beings as they continue to wallow in the ignorance and stupidity of sin, rejecting knowledge of God and Satan. It becomes quite easy to understand **[Hosea 4: 6-7]**.

To read these words of divine counsel, to acknowledge, accept them, and claim to believe them and yet not to put forth executive effort to attain to their intended purpose is to insult God and our Lord Jesus Christ, the cleansing power of his blood and his name. **[Romans 6: 19; 22], "I speak after the manner of men because of the infirmity of your flesh: for as ye have yielded your members servants to uncleanness and to iniquity unto iniquity; even so now,** at least to the extent you served sin, **yield your members servants to righteousness unto holiness". Verse 22, "But now being made free from sin, and become servants of God, ye have your fruit unto holiness, and to the end everlasting life".** Therefore, [Matthew 6: 33], "Seek ye first the kingdom of God *and his righteousness;* and all these things, verse 32 that ye have need of, shall be added unto you". [Psalms 37: 4], "Delight thyself also in the Lord; and he shall give thee the desires of thine heart".

Does this include restoring America, as there certainly seems to be a need for it? There is no doubt, a renewed long lost zeal in proclaiming the gospel in the face of the opposition of "our own countrymen" would be a good place to put our energies. There are many scriptures that express this as God's commands and will, and certainly is among **"doing always those things that please Him, [John 8: 29], and the better things that accompany salvation", [Hebrews 6:9].** This would contribute significantly to the "state of the hearts" and minds with **"prosperity of the soul", [3 John: 2]** as well as our overall living standards. Who knows, we might even learn how to **[1 Peter 1:22], "purify our souls in obeying the truth through the Spirit unto unfeigned love of the brethren and**

to love one another with a pure heart fervently". My goodness, what an enrichment of life this would be.

In **[Genesis 1:26]** we find that God made man in his own image and likeness which included a Godlike "State of the Heart" that can be reclaimed today thru God's provision of Jesus Christ as Lord and Saviour, redeeming us and reconciling us back to God for the purpose of restoring this "State of the Heart" condition to us. This Godlike "state of the heart", condition is commensurate with the **"excellence that is in them that goes away" found in [Job 4:21]**. Without this **"excellency"**, being diligently exercised, it dissipates and **"goes away, and they die "even without wisdom"**.

Though saved and born again through the blood of Jesus, this condition of God's likeness and excellency, the "State of the Heart", does not necessarily occur as an automatic result of accepting Jesus. This does requires the challenge of **[2 Timothy 2: 15], "Studying to show thyself approved unto God, a workman that needeth not to be ashamed, rightly dividing the word of truth" and the [Acts 10:35] fearing of God and working of righteousness"**. All of this is in relationship **to loving God with all you heart, soul mind, might, etc, and [Matthew 6:33] "seeking first the [installation] of the kingdom of God and his righteousness"** within you for the required state of the heart. **This is a heart that is kept with all Biblical diligence out of which comes the issues of life, [Proverbs 4:23]**. This all is required along with, and is a significant part of **"being saved by grace"**.

God gives us some real insight into the result of man's abdication of his **[Genesis 1:26]** God given dominion authority over the works of his hands, **[Psalms 8: 3-9]**. It can be accurately referred to as Satan usurping the God given power and authority of man; in essence, stealing it through deception.

To a large extent this is correct, but then as now, it can only happen if man abdicates this authority, once again, by being deceived, which those who are rebellious and disobedient have already done by such rebellion and disobedience. Jesus paid the redeeming price, not only for man's transgression but also for the returning of his creation back into the control of the **"glorious liberty of the children of God", [Romans 8: 19-23].**

Obviously this portion of scripture has future reference to it, but when we finally develop to the point where **"sin has no more dominion over us", grace having displaced the law: [Romans 6: 14],** surely this will be of great benefit to our land as well, to be applied today. The application of stupidity in the pursuit and practice of sin is what has brought destruction, spiritually and physically to our nation its people, indeed the world.

A **"lack of knowledge"** about our enemy, how he operates, his commitment to destruction; together with our lack of zeal, courage, and intelligence to enlist God's help in putting and end to his destructive methods in our own lives, our marriages, families, churches, and nation, has left us exposed to additional deceptions. We must have a renewed, conscientious look and consideration of God's **APPLIED WORD** in our lives for its cleansing effect, **[John 15: 3].**

But we will wait in hope of God's fulfilling his agenda for earth as we haven't done to good with the agenda God delivered to us. The "State of the Heart" of the Christian family, in a general sense, has not faired to well. There were, thankfully, individuals who as pillars of faith, were able to provide enough spiritual stability to keep the church going in its general intended direction. There were, however, some *"gates of hell"* established thru disunity: disunity of course being one of the main ones, along with disobedience and rebellion on an individual level, among and within the various denominations.

These "gates" have hindered to a great extent the absolute spiritual development and advancement of the church. This was the result of man attempting to build the church without adequate submission to God and his counsel. **[Psalms 127:1],"Except the Lord build the house, they labor in vain that build it".** Consequently, today we have "churches" that have embraced thoughts and ways totally contrary to Biblical directives for righteousness, holiness, and spiritual virtue. Jesus witnessed this and announced in **[Matthew 16:18] that he was going to build his own church against which these gates of hell,** *man made or devil imposed*, **could not prevail.** If you are looking for a church to attend, may I suggest this one. Attendance is however, more of an abiding consistently, taking up residence, than a periodic putting in an appearance.

The church has always had many problems of various sorts, all resulting from sin, in any one of its many forms and manifestations. This is simply because man is involved, which by necessity of fulfillment of God's plan, he must be. Nevertheless, **[Job 5: 6-7], "Although affliction cometh not forth of the dust, neither doth trouble spring out of the ground; Yet man is born unto trouble, as the sparks fly upward". [Isaiah 50: 11], "Behold, all ye that kindle a fire; that compass yourselves about with sparks: walk in the light of your fire, and in the sparks that ye have kindled. This shall ye have of mine hand; ye shall lie down in sorrow".** Man, even with God's help, just can't seem to keep his head above the troubled waters. When we enlist the Lord's assistance, maybe we should learn to cooperate with the directions he provides us to keep our fat out of the fire instead of expecting him to approve and cooperate with our wishes and desires: is there no end to man's stupidity?

It has always been thus, and our modern churches are simply an extension of what has always been, **[Ecclesiastes 1: 9], "The thing that hath been, it is that which shall be; and that which is done is that which shall be done: and there is no new thing under the sun"**, except it has progressively gotten worse. This is testimony to the expansion of man's idiocy and stupidity in his pursuit and embracing of sin and iniquity, the whole scale destruction of himself; **[Hosea 4: 6-7], verse 7, "As they were increased, so they sinned against me: therefore will I change their glory into shame"**.

As disgusting as it is, we really can't blame the world for their transgressions when we, having God's Word of counsel for direction and building of life, families, and nations, can't seem to keep our own houses in Biblical order. A short scripture in **[1 Corinthians 14: 40], "Let all things be done decently and in order"**, must not be restricted to a teaching of the operation of tongues in the church, but must, by necessity, be extended to **"ALL THINGS"** that have to do with human conversation, conduct, and behavior.

These things must, for the benefit and well being of all, including God's pleasure, be done under the Biblical directives of **"decently an in order"**. **[1 Corinthians 10: 31], "Whether therefore ye eat, or drink, or *whatsoever ye do, DO ALL to the glory of God*"**. **[Acts 17: 28], "For in him we live, and move, and have our being; as certain also of your own poets have said, for we are also His offspring"**.

A life of diligent obedience to Biblical principles and counsel, even without a deep belief in God would pay beautiful dividends. It won't save your soul, but at least your time on this earth will take on the characteristics of a life rather than mere existence. This would even be an improvement in many of our church families, thus our churches. It might even have a positive impact on our wayward leadership and nation. Wherever and by whomever it may be implemented, it will be a "win, win", situation. Try it, you'll like it. Only God knows the extent of blessings to follow such conduct. If you're a curious sort at all, give it a try. Just remember the source of these Biblical principles and instructions that you are encouraged to use in your every day life and give Him thanks along the way.

The state of the heart outside the Christian family, due to its ever increasing evil abundance, has been, and continues to be, absolutely disastrous, and our beloved nation and her people are paying a horrible price for such idiocy. Once again, there are scriptures that apply that need repeating for emphasis of essential knowledge, such as; **[Hosea 4: 7]**, **"As they increased, so they sinned against me: therefore will I change their glory into shame"**.

America is experiencing this shamefulness today she has brought on herself, not at the hands of foreign powers, but at the internal rejection of God and his power to save and deliver, **[2 Chronicles 7: 14]**, victimizing herself by her own self imposed ignorance and idiocy. Though the principle was recorded thousands of years ago, it still bears its truthful, bitter fruit, **[Hosea 4: 6]**, **"My people are destroyed for lack of knowledge: because thou hast rejected knowledge, I will also reject thee that thou halt be no priest to me: seeing thou hast forgotten the law of thy God, I will also forget thy children"**.

This principle, though primarily and originally given to the Israelites, applies to all men everywhere for all time. It, as the rest of God's Word, is still in force and relevant. No part of it can ever be rescinded, and supersedes anything and everything man can bring in opposition against it including the "supreme" court with it's erroneous, contemptible efforts to rule and reign in God's stead through their attempts to "form weapons against it's truth and absolutes", **[Isaiah 54:17], [Psalms 1: 4-6; 2]**. This certainly includes their imposition of the "separation of church and state" which has "legally" crippled the church's effectiveness to the people, and sealed the fate of the state by excommunicating God and his word from the public square. Indeed, **what fools ye mortals be.**

Though a proper state of the heart is important to all, it is especially essential for leaders, as they are the ones who must serve as examples to teach and condition those who come after them that will eventually fill their positions of leadership. When I refer to a "proper state of the heart" I must emphasize that which is founded exterior to man's evil nature which tends to his own demise. There is only one source where this proper life giving instruction, counsel, and strength can be found, and that is in Almighty God through Jesus Christ, the *Living Word,* **[John 1: 1-2,14], "In the beginning was the Word and the Word was with God, and the Word was God. The same was in the beginning with God. Vs.14, "and the Word was made flesh, and dwelt among us, and we beheld his glory, the glory as of the only begotten of the Father, full of grace and truth".**

God and God alone has what man needs to live and love and have his being according to God's own design for growth, development, and overall prosperity for, not only man but for God's entire creation. The world and certainly America is manifest proof of this through man's excommunication of God, and is evidenced by the decrepit condition of humanity and the world they have polluted by means of their sin and abominations. Thank God for the "few" exceptions, **[Matthew 7:14; Luke 13:24]**, who have been true to their calling and have maintained the truth, counsel, and direction of God's Word. These, by God's grace, have sustained the brightness of their light and the savor of their saltiness. They have shown the way and preserved many within God's care.

Unfortunately America has many "leaders" in various places of influence who have chosen **death and cursing, [Deuteronomy 30:19] rather than life and blessing,** and are continually in the process of contaminating the nation with their foolish choices in opposition to God and his truth. They are somewhat reminiscent of the three classes of persons found in **[Matthew 23], scribes, Pharisee's, and hypocrites,** who neither enter into God's kingdom and go to great lengths to prevent others from going in as well, **vs., 13.**

All this anti-Bible, anti-God, anti-Christian religion being imposed by pseudo authorities is robbing the American public of the wisdom, knowledge, and understanding that is needed to prevent eventual destruction, which as we can see in America today, is well on its way. It doesn't take much intelligence to see our beloved America today is in more of a condition of digression than it is progression, especially in a correct spiritual sense, which in reality forms the foundation for everything else.

If America is to be restored to her former glory, it is essential to realize it will only occur on the foundation of a people who have set themselves in obedience to God to **"Resurrect the Excellency"** that was originally created within them. This must be done, not to restore America, but to bring glory to God, which is the only condition on which America could be restored. The restoring of "spiritual" America must precede any attempt to reclaim our heritage, for our heritage consists of, and is founded on a Biblical spiritual heritage. Deny this, as is being done in our courts, and we bring destruction on ourselves, for to deny this is to choose death and cursing, **[Deuteronomy 30: 19-20]**

NOTES

VI.   BASIC VALUES

The questions concerning the difference and viability of religious beliefs should not be based only on the differences themselves in what or whom we believe. We must consider, what are the temporal and eternal results, effects, benefits, and rewards that those beliefs in a particular religion will produce for the overall well being of the adherents. Or are there penalties to be incurred for the opposers of such religious beliefs and practices? This must be done to determine the viability and credibility of a religious system and acceptability of its supposed or actual founders or authors. What is the nature of these different founders or authors?

Their writings, or supposed writings, if any, will expose their character and nature. Were they self created and existent exterior of man and outside of mans own imaginations, or are they the product of mans hands and imaginations, therefore less than, and inferior to man himself? Are they alive and good or are they imaginary, dead, or otherwise incapable of being good or beneficial to those who created and believe in them? All this information should be gathered and analyzed to awaken the minds and awareness of the people to the **"goodness of God that leads to repentance", [Romans 2: 4], thus bringing the people into a wholesome relationship with this majestic God of creation, love, and benevolence, who is able to honor and reward their efforts of faith and conduct.**

The gathering and analyzing of this information may well be a problem in itself, the gathering being one thing, but the analyzing being an entirely different matter. Unless all people doing the analyzing are of the same mind, in this case having to do with Bible based and orientated information, there will arise differences of opinions concerning the proper interpretation and translations of the "gathered material". We Christians see this among our own, in many cases, denominations, where conflicts arise in spite of the gathered information on the table is comprised of the same Bible.

The concept of the command to; **[Philippians 1: 2],"Fulfill ye my joy, that ye be likeminded, having the same love, being of one accord, of one mind"**, seems to have eluded us somehow. How can Christians be the answer to Jesus' prayer for unity in **[John 17]** unless we put forth executive effort to reclaim and embrace this essential principle for the glory and honor of God and our own benefit that follows and is a result of obedience? **[Psalms 133: 1[; "Behold, how good and how pleasant it is for brethren to dwell together in unity".** Unity of what, if not purpose: and that to bring glory, honour, praise, and pleasure to God. I am not surprised to find a scripture in the Bible such as **[1 Peter 4: 17], "For the time is come that judgment must begin at the house of God: and if it first begin at us, what shall the end be of them that obey not the gospel of God"?** Could the disunity that abounds among the brethren of the various denominations in "the house of God" be one of the reasons that **"judgment begins at us"** who claim to be Christians and **"have the mind of Christ" [2 Corinthians 2: 16]**? It would seem as though there is much room for soul searching here. Much more could be said on this subject, but this should suffice for now.

It is folly to blindly follow some entity and give allegiance to it just because someone said so without showing sufficient reason and evidence for doing so. It is imperative that some intensive investigation and in-depth study be made to determine the validity of some entity that so far has failed to prove itself to even be worthy of serious consideration. We have experienced some tragic situations where people were led astray and died because of some questionable charismatic individual convincing them to follow them. There are several of these cases on record as well as recorded in the Bible for our warning and admonition.

To believe and have faith in something is a waste of time and effort unless that something is able to, and will reward those who believe and have faith in it, for the belief and faith thus exercised. To conjure up or create an imagined entity that is incapable of responding and fulfilling the benevolent responsibilities of an author or founder of a religious system; and then worship or follow that entity is to destroy oneself in the blinding to the reality of the destruction that awaits them. Man must exercise enough intelligence to determine whether or not that to which he dedicates his being and consecrates his loyalties has proven itself as worthy of his devotion and lifetime commitment. This is extremely difficult for the person who has been conscientiously indoctrinated in error from birth. In some cultures to break away from this established error is only done under the threat of death.

Does the ideology or entity in question provide a system of rewards and benefits for allegiance to it, or does it simply leave you facing death and destruction whether or not you believe in it, regardless of the intensity of your devotion to it? Man must realize that, being made in the image and likeness of God, by God Himself, he is himself of infinitely greater value and worth than any imagined, conjured up, or pseudo god that is brought on the scene. **[Psalms 8: 4-5; Hebrews 2:6], "What is man, that thou art mindful of him? And the son of man, that thou visitest him? For thou hast made him a little lower than the angels, [of himself]** *and hast crowned him with glory and honour".*

To have faith in something is an exercise of futility unless that something can and will honor that faith so exercised. To exercise faith for the sake of faith is hopeless without an object or entity that can and will respond favorably toward that faith. I have heard it said that it makes no difference what a person believes as long as they believe strong enough.

This sounds like something man would conjure up in his own feeble little mind in an unsuccessful attempt to avoid God, remaining without that which is required for life and living; intelligence, wisdom, understanding, knowledge and some plain common sense and sound reasoning. Once again **"what fools ye mortals be"**

It is important to realize that God has his own agenda which He will, without fail, bring to pass in a way and timing of his own choosing regardless of man's futile attempts to circumvent him. Man has nothing of more importance in his life than to make sure he is on the positive, correct side of God's, set in place, agenda. To disregard this and consider it of a lesser to no importance is to insult God's integrity and majesty, and doom oneself to a devils hell. This would manifest a total lack of wisdom and intelligence, which equates to idiocy and stupidity. God has given us all we need to avert such disaster, **[2 Peter 1: 2-3], "Grace and peace be multiplied to you through the *knowledge* of God, and of Jesus our Lord, According as his divine power hath given unto us all things that pertain unto life and godliness, through the knowledge of him that hath called us to glory and virtue".**

Man has been notorious for attempting to establish a system or method of making an end run around God to get to the rewards that are only provided by God; that he can obtain only by submitting himself to God. In man's stupor of idiocy, he can't even comprehend **[Romans 2:4], "it is the goodness of**

God that leads to repentance". He seems totally oblivious of what God declares to be sin, and cares nothing for the repentance needed in order to gain God's favor unto redemption and reconciliation and then on to the "benefits" and "rewards", **[Hebrews 11:6],** to be administered at God's loving discretion to **"them that diligently seek him in obedience to his word"**.

It seems as though Satan's greatest coup is the deceiving of man into believing he can, in his paltry, minute, little self, invent and create false gods that can provide benefits for him that he is incapable of providing for himself. Thus do they incur Almighty God's wrath unto their own destruction. There are many scriptures throughout God's Word admonishing man to love and serve Him only and **"have no other gods before him"** **[Exodus 20: 3; Matthew 4: 10; Luke 4:8].**

These false gods and religions of the world, there are many of them "evil inventions", every since the beginning of their inceptions and following; have provided nothing but degradation, death, and destruction for their founders and adherents. They are graphic examples of **"the blind leading the blind"** principle. They can provide no viable promises for fulfillment of good. They have only those falsehoods advanced by the deceptive founders, promoters and, or leaders of such religions, including secular humanism.

Any "religion" that does not and cannot declare and provide for immediate, temporal, and the assurance of eternal benefits for the whole person, based on **"great and precious promises"**, common sense and sound reasoning, should be promptly rejected. If it does not have an underlying, supporting, base and condition of love, well being, and promotion for all, it is not worthy of consideration. Residing within this condition of love for the promotion of all is the worthy concept of righteousness, purity, and holiness, which is essential to the establishing, maintaining, and promotion of life and unto life more abundantly for all who will accept this **"new and living way" [Hebrews 10:20].** It would seem that all men everywhere would desire and pursue this for **themselves and their "seed", [Deuteronomy 30:19],** their descendents. As simple as the concept is, it is amazing that the multitudes lack the common sense and desire to accept it, especially those to whom it has been made known.

Man is not naturally endowed with the intelligence and common sense unto progression within himself: without some exterior source, outside himself, to supply, teach, and lead, in these areas. He remains somewhat of a bungling idiot, and proves it by rejecting and despising such assistance as is provided to him by God himself. If man were naturally endowed with such, we would have no need of institutions of education from the elementary to the unending progression needed for both the general and specific things of life. Most of us even had to learn to feed ourselves and had trouble doing that. There is an analogy here concerning learning how to feed ourselves with that which God has provided for our well being and enrichment of life. See if you can figure it out. Possibly your pastor can assist you.

It is quite apparent that, even with these institutions of higher education, their influences, input, and training, this basic intelligence that is so necessary to a harmonious and beneficial world and community "togetherness" is sadly lacking due to the whole scale rejection of the source of Godly intelligence, wisdom, and understanding. Who is to blame; we are, because we haven't even the common sense to discern between good and evil, that which pleases God, and is beneficial to us, versus that which is destructive. It never ceases to amaze me that, even with God's direction, counsel, and command, man will, overwhelmingly, choose death and cursing in preference to life and blessing. He will, by a great majority of numbers, choose ideologies, concepts, beliefs, and religions that are contrary to this life and blessing abundance that God has made available to us. I am constantly, by man's ignorance, rebellion, and stupidity, reminded of William Shakespeare's immortal words **"What fools ye mortals be"**.

I believe ole Willie must have taken his cue from **[Proverbs 1:7], "The fear of the Lord is the beginning of knowledge: but fools despise wisdom and instruction"**. Thus we are given a Biblical description of those who reject and despise wisdom, knowledge, instruction, understanding, and yes, God ordained "intelligence" with just plain common sense, which in the exercise thereof, has the ability to alleviate many problems such as are common to man in his "foolishness". **[Job 5: 7], "Yet man is born unto trouble, as the sparks fly upward"** as even common sense is in short supply and continues to diminish at an ever increasing rate, **[Hosea 4: 6-7], verse 7, "As they were increased, so they sinned against me: therefore I will change their glory into shame"**. What a sad, unnecessary indictment against this once God fearing, God honoring nation that American's have brought on themselves. The remedy still remains available but still remains rejected. Indeed, **"What fools ye mortals be"**.

If all men were from a common point presented with the conglomeration of religions and their various beliefs and the benefits and rewards, if any, to analyze before choosing; there is no doubt but what we would be living in a better world. We are not presented with that opportunity however, as young minds are usually conditioned to the prevailing religious beliefs and concepts of their homeland, at a very young age, if there be any religion there at all. Erroneous, contrary beliefs thus driven into the young hearts and minds bear the bitter fruits of evil and are generally more harmful than none at all. These erroneous contrary beliefs are the source of "the inventions of evil things", **[Romans 1: 29-31]** produced by evil thoughts and thinking that like Lucifer are a product of "the iniquity that is found in us", **"But God" [Ephesians 2:4-10].**

This is a result of societies where there has been no intelligent leadership, counsel of righteousness, or holiness of thought and conduct to the prevention of such stupidity and ignorance. These beliefs are a result of no religion at all, or misguided, wrongfully imposed religious input. This whole scenario has had a severe tendency to enslave the adherents to harmful practices rather than allow them the freedom to choose, initiate, and practice wholesome Bible taught, life giving pursuits. Once again, this whole evil scenario of rebellion against God's provision of "good", **[Romans 2: 4-6],** is the reason entire nations and societies have disappeared and exist now only in historical records with only an occasional appearance as proof of their presence and subsequent demise in archaeological discoveries.

We in America are now faced with the destructive concept of "the separation of church and state" which is being "religiously" demanded and promoted by the state, and is detrimental to the very well being, life, and continuation, of America, including especially those who espouse such idiocy. They would never admit to it being a religion, as that would bring it under the heading of a "church" which they have banned. But, it is, however, "religiously" demanded and promoted by the state and its proponents; and the populace is, "by constitutional law", thus deceived, conned, and forced to comply with it regardless of how erroneous and ill-conceived it is.

There is, thank God, a few individual thinkers who do not adhere to mans erroneous governmental thinking and thoughts concerning God's commission to the "church" with its Godly **[Galatians 5:22-23] attributes, against which there is no law;** except by mans idiocy. Unfortunately, we of the church world, through our own idiocy, have allowed the element of sinful man to make the laws and demand obedience to them. This so called "law of the land" has proved to be a poor substitute for that which God provided for his creation in his Word of Truth and Absolutes for counsel, guidance, and direction of the world's people. Our nation is graphically showing the adverse effects of that "abdication of authority". Adam may have been the first to be seduced by this deception to the abdication of God given authority, but he certainly was not the last. It is amazing that those to whom God gave dominion authority were, and are, so quick and willing to give it up to those who oppose God, his truth, and absolutes.

We must ask ourselves; what is the condition of being that provides for the safe, healthy, constructive development of minds and lives according to God's standards and values versus the deceptive things that are harmful and destructive? The answer to this question will involve considerable intelligent thought, study, and meditation, and maybe best answered by a scripture, **[Matthew 5:6], "Blessed are they which do hunger and thirst after righteousness: for they shall be filled"**. Let's include some other scriptures with this, as it is essential that we all get a good understanding of what "righteousness" is comprised of.

The hungering and thirsting implies an intense desire that will not be denied, such as **"setting your affection"**, **[Colossians 3:2], "Set your affection on things above, not on things on earth"**. The "things above" are the things of which righteousness is composed, and this "above", is the location and source from which righteousness originated and continues to originate as the source of what is correct, right, and holy for the satisfying of the hungering, thirsting soul, heart and mind. This location and source can correctly be considered as ***"the heart of God"***, **"for from the abundance of the heart, the mouth speaketh"**. For from the abundance of his heart, God has provided us guidance, counsel, and provision that is beyond price.

[2 Peter 3:13], "Nevertheless we, according to his promises, look for new heavens and a new earth, wherein dwelleth righteousness". Therefore, [Matthew 6:33], "seek ye first, above and in preference to everything else, the kingdom of God AND his righteousness, and all these things, which the Father knows you have need of, shall be added unto you". [John 3:16]: "For God so loved the world that he gave His only begotten Son, that whosoever believeth in Him should not perish, but have everlasting life": fulfilling the requirements of love. God gave so that we might live and have life and life more abundantly through Christ Jesus. This place **"wherein dwelleth righteousness"** must begin to take shape in our hearts and minds today as characteristic of "the new, the inner; the Christlike man". All he is asking us to do is to love as he loved, meet the demands of that love, and let him take care of the paydays, and of course, the fringe benefits which are beyond our comprehension.

In this unscrupulous world, when a person gets a job, they need to be concerned about the extent of their wages plus the fringe benefits lest some dishonest person swindle them out of their earnings. It seems like this is an every day occurrence in corporate America these days. In God's economy we can trust him to do what he has promised while we turn our full attention and energies to the **"working of righteousness"**. **[Acts 10:34-35], "Then Peter opened his mouth and said, of a truth I perceive that God is no respecter of persons: But, [however,** regardless], in every nation he that feareth him and WORKETH RIGHTEOUSNESS is accepted with him".

Recently a brother and I were visiting and he was telling me of a sermon he gave one Sunday about having favor with God. This "fearing, reverencing, and honoring" of God and working of the righteousness required by love will insure this "favor" and keep us on the right side, "the redeemed" side of God's agenda. It is important that we spend quality time in study and meditation concerning these things, as even in some Christian circles, the depth of understanding of love, righteousness and the kingdom of God, **"the things above"**, is somewhat lacking.

[Proverbs 4:7], "Wisdom is the principal thing; therefore get wisdom: and with all thy getting get understanding". Wisdom, understanding, knowledge, intelligence, common sense, a renewed mind, a prosperous soul, a contrite heart: these are things not purchased at the local mall or supermarket, neither with big bucks or credit cards. Neither are the things that must be established and promoted, such as successful lives, marriages, families, wholesome safe communities, nor well educated, trained, and contributive children: all these things that are necessary to the stability of a nation, purchased in such a manner.

These things all proceed from the principles of God's word which is a revealing of his own heart. **[Luke 6:45], "A good man out of the good treasure of his heart bringeth forth that which is good.** This gives us a clue as to the origin of **"the goodness of God that leadeth men to repentance" [Romans 2:4]; "and an evil man out of the evil treasure of his heart bringeth forth that which is evil: for out of the abundance of the heart the mouth speaketh", the mind thinketh and the hand doeth.** Please excuse this little Edwards add on.

With this principle of the abundance of the heart being the source of the words spoken; if you wish to know God's heart, STUDY HIS WORD. If you want to know God's will generally or specifically, *study his word.* The main reason people complain that they just can't find God's will for their life is because God's will doesn't match up with their will, or what they want. God's will for our lives is based on what we need.

Our will is based on what we want, which is controlled by our feelings and emotions which are primarily generated out of *"affections being set on the things of this earth"*. There are no doubt exceptions to this as we mature in Christ, but this seems to be the general trend. Wants are not bad if they are expressed in conjunction with our needs as outlined in God's Word of truth; our three basic needs being Wisdom, Knowledge, and Understanding.

Modern technology has produced many things that were and are needed in our expanding population, but the need for the **"things above"** have not and cannot be provided, replaced or substituted by things of our modern technology. Nevertheless, they may at times and under certain circumstances be facilitated with the proper use of wisdom and discretion. The other side of the coin is, that in the promotion of Biblical principles, there are things of this earth that are essential to the facilitation of such promotion. Spiritual food and material provision are both vital to life and living.

In addition to things needed for development and enrichment, this technology has produced many other things for people to desire and want including credit cards, which unfortunately are seldom used with wisdom and discretion. It is not the cards that have caused the problems, but the lack of practical Biblical taught principles of wisdom, knowledge understanding, discretion, etc., with the execution thereof.

[Ecclesiastes 7: 12], "For wisdom is a defense, and money is a defense: but the excellency of knowledge is, that wisdom giveth life to them that have it". [Proverbs 22: 7], "The rich ruleth over the poor, and the borrower is servant to the lender". Unfortunately, unless considerable discretion, which is in short supply these days, is diligently taught, slavery rather than just being a servant, due to debt, is a common occurrence.

It makes me wonder if the teaching of these practical principles would be forbidden in our schools because they are Bible principles and the Bible, God's Word, is the basic instruction and training manual of the church, thus violating the so called "separation of church and state" fallacy. It is not hard to see that God in his fullness is as practical as he is spiritual; and that man is as impractical as he is stupid.

Though it may seem like it, I am not implying here that the unsaved, secular man has no propensity for developing common sense. Being made in the image and likeness of God, there is a remnant of the original abilities left after the Garden of Eden experience, by God's grace, even in the unregenerate being. This remnant is the ability to develop other abilities which man has accomplished to a great extent.

The evolutionism monkeyists know nothing of this. All this learning with its great accomplishments, however, is no substitute for being "born again" and establishing intimacy with God through Jesus Christ. With all the astounding accomplishments and advancements man has made through the learning, gaining, and application of knowledge, he is sadly lacking in his attainment to the beginning of wisdom that starts with the **"fearing and reverencing of God", [Psalms 111:10; Proverbs 1:7].**

There are, of course, the few exceptions that go through the strait gate and walk the narrow way that leads unto life, as opposed to the larger multitude **"that go through the wide gate and walk the broad way that leads to destruction", [Matthew 7:13-14].** These non-exceptions are those who have cast the word of God behind their backs, and despised the values and standards of God's word, rejected his righteous counsel unto salvation and **"the things that accompany salvation" [Hebrews 6:9].** Thank God for the remnant, the exceptions who by the grace of God, embrace, study, and practice, these values and standards, **serving the Lord their God with joyfulness and gladness of heart for the abundance of all things, [Deuteronomy 28:47].**

NOTES

NOTES

VII. PERSONAL OBSERVATION

In my personal observations of humanity, I am convinced that for the most part, humanity consists of ignorance, stupidity, and foolishness. The condition of our world, and indeed our own nation is graphic testimony to that fact. There are those, however, with a questionable sense of loyalty to a rapidly failing governmental system that is primarily at fault for the dismantling of our great nation, who will disagree with me.

There are extensive records and accounts in God's Word testifying to the demise of kingdoms, governments, and nations who suffered horribly by following leaders who "caused the whole nation to sin" by there un-Godly corrupt leadership. Regardless, there are exceptions, a remnant, to use Bible terminology, who have great regard for God, his word, his wisdom, etc, which include his provision of this bountiful land. I like to think of myself as one of those exceptions of which there are many, but few in comparison to the multitudes who are not among the exceptions.

I am, nevertheless, aware of the fact that even a committed exception must **[Proverbs 4:23], "Keep thy heart with all diligence; for out of it are the issues of life"**, lest in an unguarded moment one slip back into the issues of death that God in his mercy and grace provided deliverance from. We human beings, even though saved have a propensity to do that, **[1 Peter 5: 8], "Be sober, be vigilant; because your adversary the devil, as a roaring lion, walketh about, seeking whom he may devour"**. Rest assured, if you are a Christian, you are his target, and there are many among *"our own countrymen"* who are his willing assistants, his henchmen, who are seeking your downfall.

The Christian is always subject to attack; if not directly from the devil himself, then through a multitude of his willing assistants, who may well be among the Christian's own "countrymen" of which Paul speaks of in his journeys, **[2 Corinthians 11: 26], "In journeys often, in perils of waters, in perils of robbers,** *in perils by mine own countrymen,* **in perils by the heathen, in perils in the city, in perils in the wilderness, in perils in the sea,** *in perils among false brethren".*

Though the diligently kept and guarded heart issues forth life; the un-kept, unguarded heart issues forth death and cursing. Thank God for his provision of deliverance from these dungeons of existence and prisons of survival where mankind insists on plodding through their allotted time on earth doing things their own way in profound rejection of God and his counsel. These are those that go through the **"wide gate and struggle along the broad way that leads to destruction" [Matthew 17:13],** those who have **[Deuteronomy 30:19], chosen death and cursing instead of life and blessing, and passing such choice on to their "seed".** So much for the intelligence of the vast majority of humanity!

Then there is the minority, who are a minority in number only, the exceptions, the remnant, the few that go through the strait gate and travel the narrow way that leads to life everlasting, **[Matthew 7: 13-14].** These, who have by embracing God's eternal provision of salvation and reconciliation through Jesus Christ, have been delivered from those dungeons and prisons of darkness, despair, and death into the light of life and life more abundantly.

These may be a minority in number, but are a majority in quality due to their Godly influence on society, and thus the nation. This is all based on intelligent choice, or possibly a choice prompted by desperation to escape from some meager, pointless existence, but nevertheless the choice to **[Mark 1:15]**, **"repent and believe the gospel"**, *choosing life and blessing for themselves and their "seed"* in obedience to God's command to make such a choice, **[Deuteronomy 30: 19]**. Isn't it amazing that mankind is so deficient in intelligence that he has to be told to choose life and blessing instead of death and cursing, and given viable reasons for doing so to induce him to make the correct choice?

Even with all this, the multitudes still fail to make that choice. Jesus said **"I have come that ye might have life and that ye might have life more abundantly" [John 10: 10]**. This raises the question: What does the life that God has commanded us to choose consist of and imply? The apparent, over all answer to this is the blessings, benefits, and rewards, temporal, and eternal which are the results of making this correct choice.

Now it is up to the individual to study to identify the specific, one at a time, blessings that are implied here for the purpose of blending our life with them all. This will give us an idea of what the divine nature of God is all about, and give us many profitable and prosperous hours of meditation and study with wonderful discoveries, if we so choose to intelligently indulge ourselves.

This begins the journey of life, the embracing of this provision of God, this-Saviour, King, and Friend, Jesus, the living fulfillment of God's plan for all mankind. **[Ephesians 2:8], "For by grace are ye saved by faith and not of yourselves, it is the gift of God".** It is neither my intent nor desire to waste time on the subject of the despair and destruction of life through sin and rebellion against God; we've all had enough of this, but to get on with the life and life more abundantly of exploration and development in Jesus.

As we proceed in this study, meditating, learning, practicing, developing, and attaining to God's purpose for our lives; we will, through fulfilling **[1 Thessalonians 4:4], "possessing" our "vessels", our beings, in "sanctification and honour", with [Hebrews 6:9], "the things that accompany salvation, and [John 8:29], those things that please God",** consistently displace those things that are contrary to God's righteousness and holiness. In this manner, **the house of [Matthew 12:44] may well be swept and garnished, but it is not empty,** *but filled with sanctification and honour unto the Lord,* and the returning spirits find no refuge, nor sanctuary.

It is through this process of growing in the grace and knowledge of our Lord we will most assuredly reinstate, grasp and begin to experience the "likeness" of God that he originally designed in man but has been lost due to a lack of emphasis in exploring, discovering, and resurrecting, **[Job 4:21], "the excellency that is in them"** contained in this area of God's likeness. This is "follow thru" on the decision to choose life and blessing that we are then able to pass on to our "seed". It is important for a person to know that without Jesus Christ they are a sinner, without God they are a sinner, but they were not created this way, to be sinners. They "we", were created to be in the "image and likeness of God". Sin entered in as an "alien" invader to destroy this wonderful creation, **Ephesians 2: 1-3. [Ephesians 2: 4-10], "But God".** Study these verses to get a revelation of how loved and valued you are to God.

Satan's invasion is kind of like a virus in your computer. Satan installed it and only God's provision of a Saviour, Jesus Christ can remove and deliver us from it. But man has to want to get rid of it, otherwise, rest assured it will destroy you. **[John**

10:10], **The thief, satan, cometh not but to steal, to kill and to destroy everything that God intends for you to have and become, but Jesus came to give us life and life more abundantly,** to restore all that was lost in the "fall" when Adam first abdicated man's dominion authority.

The "likeness", this "excellency" of God, created and designed in us, not being emphasized, not being fixed in our minds to where we meditate on it and think about the wonders of it, becomes kind of an "out of sight out of mind" concept. Being somewhat lost, buried and undiscovered, it was never taught with an emphasis needed to contribute to our needed development in Christ. It does take a conscious effort, **[Psalms 1:2], to delight in it, to meditate on, and study it to become aware of it to the point of realizing the importance and value of it.** We must, through study and commitment to this "Word of God", get a vision of its necessity and value.

As the life giving value of it is realized, this realization will project us into deeper and more intense study with additional blessings, spiritual growth, and development being desired and experienced. This will not happen if a person is not interested in doing so. Such a **"vision of value"**, if presented diligently, may well encourage an otherwise disinterested person to investigate and pursue this line of Biblical thinking, and thus enjoy the results. If this is to be reintroduced into our mentality, our thinking abilities, there must definitely be an ongoing process of the *"renewing of the mind"*. It is in this **"image and likeness", [Genesis 1: 26], that the concept of "the Excellency that is in them" begins to emerge. [Job 4:21], [Psalms 1:3]**

Let's face it, man needs all the help he can get and what better place to get the help he needs than at the feet of Jesus. Man does have a bit of a problem with this as to swallowing his pride and admitting he needs help. He has developed into rather an independent critter with the idea that independence is the mark of a man. The problem with this is that in establishing his own selfish independence, he has lost sight of how much he needs to depend on God, and does in fact depend on him without even realizing it.

This receiving and enjoying God's abundance without even acknowledging God as the provider of such abundance is characteristic of humanity. Without acknowledging God as the provider, neither will man show his gratitude and give God thanks. This is an eternal problem that man neither understands nor comprehends the seriousness of, simply because he is not aware of the eternal consequences of his "selfish independence". Man may well struggle through some sort of an existence here on this earth, and if he happens to "strike it rich" he might even be able to afford and simulate something he might mistake for living, or life. At any rate his existence may well take on an easier and more enjoyable aura of survival, though not yet life to the extent God intended for him to have and enjoy.

I have a dear friend, Don Manning, who says of money; it's better to have it than not have it; it's better to have more of it than less of it, and its better to have it sooner than later. This is good if it is under the control of Godly wisdom, knowledge, and understanding, [Biblical taught principles]. **[Ecclesiastes 7:11-12], "Wisdom is good with an inheritance: and by it there is profit to them that see the sun. For wisdom is a defense, and money is a defense: BUT the *excellency* of knowledge is, that WISDOM GIVETH LIFE TO THEM THAT HAVE IT".** I think the same thing could be said and with greater emphasis and significance about Jesus. It's better, much better to have him than not to have him, it's better, much better, to have more of him in your heart than less of him, **and**

it is by all means better to have him sooner than later. This in itself is the epitome of wisdom, knowledge, understanding, and intelligence.

It is only through Jesus that that we can attain to the "image and likeness' of God and once again realize and enjoy the Godly "excellency" that is to be found only within his likeness, the likeness that God designed in us and intended for us to manifest from the beginning. I wouldn't even begin to try to describe to you the extent of this "excellency" or what it consists of but, this one thing I will say about it; it is vitally essential in the continuing and developing of Godly **"fullness"**, **[Ephesians 3: 19]** without which we cannot live as God designed us.

The very word "excellency" commands a majestic idea and attitude about it that captures attention and portrays a high standard of quality, character, and value. It has been used as a title for some dignitaries of state regardless of the character of the individual in an attempt to command respect and honor, at least for the office if not for the individual who may well have not been deserving of the title.

Nevertheless, God intended for us to possess and manifest it for his glory and honor and our eternal benefit. The significance of all this God ordained abundance to man and the love that compelled God to give his son Jesus to die so that we might be partakers of it all is absolutely mind boggling. Such love, such wondrous love that God should love us so much as to make provision for us, through the sacrifice of his Son, to change from sinner to saint, from sinners to **[2 Corinthians 5:17]**, **"new creatures in Christ saved by his amazing grace"**.

Adam abdicated the authority, position, and power that God initially gave to man, **[Ephesians 2:4-6], "But God, who is**

rich in mercy, for his great love wherewith he loved us", made provision for us to reclaim this image and likeness and resurrect the **[Job 4:21] "excellency that is in them". "Even when we were dead in sins, God hath quickened us together with Christ, [by grace are ye saved]; and hath raised us up together, and made us sit together in heavenly places in Christ Jesus"**. This was not done so that we might have a casual acquaintance with God, but to establish a loving relationship of spiritual intimacy where we can be partakers of God's own divine nature and dwell in his presence.

Thank God for the exceptions in humanity who exercise the required intelligence to accept God's offer of salvation, redemption, and reconciliation, **the choosing of life and blessing, [Deuteronomy 30: 19].**

Though the vast majority of mankind may be lost in their choice of death and cursing through the ignorance, foolishness, and stupidity of rebellion against God, it is comforting to know there is at least a minority blessed for their obedience and love for God. These are the light of the world and the salt of the earth. These are our brothers and sisters in Christ, regardless of who they are or where they might be.

VIII. ONE NATION, UNDER GOD

ONE NATION UNDER GOD: do we really understand the significance of this statement? Do we really have a proper idea, perception, or concept of who this **"GOD"** really is? Our knowledge in this area is quite lacking, do to neglect, even in many Christian circles. Outside of the Christian "religion", such knowledge is not only lacking but rejected; and in many cases despised; **[Isaiah 5: 24], "Therefore as the fire devoureth the stubble, and the flame consumeth the chaff, so their root shall be as rottenness, and their blossom shall go up as dust: BECAUSE** *they have cast away the law of the Lord of hosts, and despised the word of the Holy One of Israel".*

In consideration of who God is and his relationship to his creation, only his thoughts, his ways, his counsel, and truth, **[Isaiah 55: 8-9]**, can realistically be considered when discussion concerning the operations of his world, its peoples, and its well being are on the agenda. Only his word in reference to man, his world, his development, his conduct, his being, his behavioral patterns, and ultimately his eternal destiny can be considered for God has the final judgment in all these matters regardless of what they may be, or who says otherwise or to the contrary.

In **[Isaiah 55: 8], "God tells us that his thoughts are not our thoughts, neither are his ways our ways, Verse 9 continues, for as the heavens are higher than the earth, so are his ways higher than our ways, and his thoughts than our thoughts"**. This gives us quite a large area for accepting the challenge of growing into. There is a very basic reason for this. Ways, conduct, behavior, including our words, proceeding from **"the abundance of our heart"**, **[Luke 6:45]**, will always follow, and be a result of our line of thinking and thought processes.

If our mentality is based on proper influence and conditioning, God's counsel; the resultant lifestyle and personal culture will be based on properly formed attitudes about ourselves, the world we live in, its people, and certainly God and his fullness, whether we understand it all or not. Who we are, what we are, must be based on what God says, not on what we think according to man's inferior earth bound mentality. If we adjust our lives to the world we live in, we will never ascend to God's intended potential, thinking his thoughts, and doing things his way.

Man without God's input, even with his best intentions, will always pull you down with discouragement and deception. **[Acts 17: 28], "For in him [God] we live and move and have our being; for we are also his offspring"**. Because of this, when debate or dialogue is entered into, **[2 Corinthians 10: 5]**; we must **"cast down imaginations, and every high thing that exalteth itself against the knowledge of God, and bring into captivity every thought to the obedience of Christ"**. This takes time, determination, diligence, and much study and practice; but with God, all things are possible and the benefits and rewards are beyond our comprehension, **[Hebrews 11: 6]**.

The Christian has no choice but to discount and reject all argument that is raised against God and His Word of Truth. This we must do when we are engaged in debate, dialogue, decision making, or meditating within ourselves, even when no other person is involved. The world cannot understand this, so they consider their arguments just as viable, or even more so, than the Christian view.

As a consequence they see us as a bunch of intolerant bigots when we refuse to diversify in their direction of error. Consequently, they reject the idea of God with his truth and counsel as being any greater than theirs, even as good as theirs, or even worthy of consideration. If they are so concerned about diversity, I would invite them to diversify in God's direction of truth and absolutes. In fact in their denial of the reality of God, they completely reject the importance of God and his counsel in any discussions or dialogue.

Consequently the vast majority of dialogue and rhetoric that pours forth from this rebellious bunch, lost in a fog of their own idiocy, is completely void of any direction toward solutions to the problems they ramble on about, but in addition are totally lacking in any oratory eloquence. However a considerable amount of doubletalk that says nothing, goes nowhere, and accomplishes nothing for the good and wellbeing of mankind including themselves; but only adds some additional confusion of the issues at hand is usually forthcoming.

Any level of individual from the uneducated to the highly educated can hash over problems and dilemmas, but it is going to take a person endowed with at least some intelligence to provide and execute solutions to the existing chaotic conditions caused by lesser men. Any bungling idiot with a sledge hammer and wrecking bar in hand can tear a house down, but it takes a skilled person of proper training, skill and knowledge to build and maintain one. Our nation was built and handed to we modernists by much work and sacrifice of our forefathers, and we, in a little over two hundred years have managed, in spite of all our advancements, to nearly destroy it, let alone maintain it and improve it from a spiritual and moral standpoint. Too much violation of **[Colossians 3: 2], "Set your affection on things above, not on things on earth",** along with many other scriptures, I suspect!

If it is to be a house equipped with the beneficial spiritual furnishings necessary for its life, success, and prosperity, there must be a certain amount of Godly intelligence included along with the required wisdom, knowledge, and understanding of, **the Knowledge of the Holy; [Proverbs 9: 10-11], "The fear of the Lord is the beginning of wisdom: and the knowledge of the holy is understanding". For by me thy days shall be multiplied, and the years of thy life shall be increased".** To reject this is to labor in vain, whether it be an individual life, family, church, state, nation, or whatever, including political parties. **[Psalms 127: 1], "Except the Lord build the house, they labour in vain that build it: except the Lord keep the city the watchman waketh but in vain"** and the continual prattling of the "leaders" becomes as **"a tale told by an idiot, full of sound and fury and signifying nothing", [Shakespeare].**

It is amazing how William Shakespeare in his day so aptly described the mental, and thus the verbal content of our post-modern day with all our advancements, education, and progress; but not so amazing when you consider God's ability to equip every person to do whatever he wills. But in rebellion against God's will does America continue in her demise, degradation, and ever increasing shame, **[Hosea 4: 7], "As they increased so they sinned against me: therefore I will change their glory into shame".** She has no leaders that exercise themselves to return her to her greatness, or people who demand it, so the idiotic tale continues on, and **[Hosea 4: 6-7]** continues in it's fulfillment along with other appropriate scriptures that can well be applied for truth and accuracy.

It is this mentality in the rejection of God's truth that has brought this world, including America into total chaos and confusion, and to the brink of destruction: not from exterior sources but within. It is not only a number of our officially elected or appointed leaders in their positions and offices of authority who are to blame but also the people, with a few exceptions of course. The people, who in their own neglect of God, his thoughts and ways, have not held themselves responsible nor accountable to that which is right according to God's standards and values. Whether or not the proclamation of God's truth is rendered legal or illegal by mans determination is irrelevant.

The question is between what is right versus wrong by God's determination, although man is constantly trying to make God's word illegal by their erroneous " separation of church and state" nonsense, which it seems is aimed at the Christian religion or church. Nevertheless, only God's Word can be considered as the true authority and relied upon. **[Matthew 24 35], "Heaven and earth shall pass away, but my words shall not pass away"**. Because of negligence in pursuit of Godliness on the people's part, they have not demanded that their leaders be held accountable to these standards and values presented in God's counsel, but instead have opted for the Godless ways of their leaders.

There are signs of this changing as we are witnessing a frustration and dissatisfaction among the populace, yet both leaders and general public sharing the same mentality in resisting God's thoughts and ways, neither one realizing that God is the only answer to their dilemmas. America has degraded to the point that the general populace neither know nor understand the absolute necessity of the imposition of these Biblical standards, values, and principles for the overall health, welfare, and wellbeing, strength, and destiny of themselves, the nation and the world.

How often have we heard the reaction to a gospel message that goes something like this, **"their not going to cram**

religion down my throat". Yet these same people have been choking on the devils fare all their lives, and he has been cramming it down their throats and destroying them with it. And they will fight to the death, protecting some idiotic right to continue to indulge themselves in their self destruction while claiming to be free and enjoy themselves in the process. These people, **[Romans 1: 32], "Who knowing the judgment of God, that they which commit such things are worthy of death, not only do the same, but have pleasure in them that do them".**

Thank God, not all have done this, thank God for the few, the exceptions. It seems that every one who has any awareness and concern about the state of humanity and our country is deeply concerned about the direction our nation is going. There are those who say everything is going okay, everything is fine, don't worry about it. This is the Republican view when their administration is on top and all the problems are Democrats fault. The view is reversed when the Democrats are in office and control. Each party blaming the other for the problems and neither one accepting their role or responsibility for the part they played in bringing our wonderful nation to its knees.

Disagree with me if you will, but before you disagree too much, take a good honest look at the things that are happening within the borders of our post-modern world where man has turned his back on God and despised his word. Take an honest, hard look at the atrocities that people are committing against each other, today and everyday, in our great, grand, and noble America. America, the land of the free that is so bound in sin and iniquity that it is self destructing; America, the home of the brave where there isn't enough spiritual backbone left in our government to initiate change in favor of God and his word, even if they had the knowledge to do so. **[Hosea 4: 6], "My people are destroyed for lack of knowledge: because thou** hast rejected knowledge, I will also reject thee that thou shalt be no priest to me: seeing thou hast forgotten the law, [word] of thy God, I will also forget thy children".

It is a bit disgusting when you realize that God has provided us a way out of our self imposed problems and dilemmas through Jesus Christ and multitudes refuse to avail themselves of what God in his love has made available for them. The food we eat, the clothes we wear, the houses we build, the cars we drive, and the fuel they burn, all from the elements God created for the benefit of this ungrateful creature He made out of the dust of the ground, and give dominion over it all.

And then God gave man the ability to learn and develop the abilities to accomplish all these things, and the majority of these rebellious ungrateful wretches won't even take the time to express their gratitude and thank him for this vast supply, or even acknowledge that He exists. **[Genesis 1: 31], "And God saw every thing that he had made, and behold, it was *very good*. And the evening and the morning were the sixth day".**

As to the problems and troubles we witness daily throughout our America, I will leave the details of that up to the individual reader to do their own research on this. I won't even try to name all these transgressions and abominations as there are so many and utterly disgusting and increasing in numbers and intensity daily among a people that claim to be intelligent; **[Hosea 4: 7],"As they increased, so they sinned against me: therefore I will change their glory into shame".**

Just turn on your television to the news channels and watch between the commercials. They are committed to providing you with accounts of all the murder, riot, rape, rebellion, etc, etc, and whatever else is available for them to take advantage of to sell news to keep their ratings up.

You will hear considerable rhetoric and dialogue about the problems that are plaguing our nation, but never any information toward direction, correction, and solution to these problems. There are basically two reasons for this. The first reason is because the solutions to all these troubles are of "spiritual" Godly substance and foundation, and unknown to the majority of those who could make a difference in our government. The second is because of the erroneous additional abomination of the "separation of church and state" which has boiled down to a separation of God and people: they have rendered the whole subject of God, his Christ, and his word unconstitutional, therefore illegal and, with the exception of a few, the people have accepted this garbage. God never intended for his "state" government to be a separate part of his kingdom apart from the church, but in harmony with the church keeping kingdom decency and order of righteousness and holiness according to his own Bible values and standards, the principles revealed in his word.

Beside all this, it isn't profitable for T. V. ratings. So here we are today with a nation that God set in place and He isn't even allowed a voice in its operation and management. Really, how stupid can people get, and then lay claims to intelligence? Our Supreme Court and governmental officials must be very proud of themselves for setting the stage for the destruction of this great nation by excommunicating God and His Word of Truth, with the population participating in their willingness of being the blind following the blind.

Outside of God's Word and counsel, there is no correction for our dilemmas, or the intelligence to facilitate any. If the non-Christian elements of this world have found any, let them present it as proof that they are correct in their rebellion against God. They neither know nor care what the solution is, but are bound and trapped by the erroneous "separation of church and state" and political correctness fallacy in a nonsensical attempt to discredit God and his word.

This has been characterizing America for far to long, and the proponents of this Godless abomination are among America's worst and most devious enemies; as Paul puts it in **[2 Corinthians 11: 26], "mine own countrymen"** causing her destruction from within her own household, **[Matthew 10: 36[, "And a mans foes shall be they of his own household"**. Thank God there is a whole realm of truth outside of "political correctness", which is nothing other than that described as **"holding, binding, the truth in unrighteousness", [Romans 1: 18]**.

God help us to wake up, leaders and all. People need to wake up and demand competent leaders who will take steps to return, and encourage the return to the basic Biblical principles on which this nation was founded, the principles of the Christian religion. However, the people, if they ever hope to save themselves as well as their nation must return to these principles which both leaders and the populace have rejected to their own destruction.

There must be a whole scale return to God. Nations have prospered when they have repented and returned in obedience to God, **[2 Chronicles 7: 14],** and were destroyed when they refused. America will be granted no exception to this, and neither the leaders nor the ones being led seem to understand this. The return to the Bible based the Christian "religion" with its truth and absolutes, is an absolute necessity if America is to have any hope in surviving her crisis. This is a truth and principle that applies to individuals, marriages, on to and including nations and countries.

The inclusion of the multitude of other religions for the sake of diversity, tolerance, and political correctness is an insult to God. It may be important to the politically correct crowd, but I doubt that God is impressed and certainly not intimidated. **[Matthew 4: 10], "Thou shalt worship the Lord thy God, and him only shalt thou serve". [Exodus 20: 3]; "Thou shalt have no other god's before me".** This is not merely a suggestion. It is a commandment reiterated in **[Matthew 22: 37-39], "Jesus said, thou shalt love the Lord thy God with all thy heart, with all thy soul, and with all thy mind. Vs. 38, This is the first and great commandment. Vs. 39, And the second is like unto it, Thou shalt love thy neighbor as thyself".**

This "love" can only be obtained through God's established principle's, and this concept of loving our neighbors as ourselves seems to be another hurdle we human beings are having a tough time getting over. The "freedom of religion" idea with allegiance to whatever man wished to consider as a god is an evil invention of man prompted by his father the devil in an attempt to discredit God, his Word, and his program of redemption, and was profoundly condemned by God from the beginning, but is having a devastating affect on all mankind because of mans stupidity of rebellion. **[John 14: 6], "Jesus saith, I am the way, the truth, and the life: no man cometh to the Father, but by me".**

Contrary to human reasoning, not all "religious" roads lead to heaven. It is impossible, for the sake of diversity, tolerance, and more political correctness, to mix the impure with the pure and expect the pure to remain pure. A good friend, sincere as he was, once told me, diversity is what made this country great. Without hesitation I replied, diversity is what is destroying this country.

What man regards as greatness is most certainly different and considerably less than God's concept of greatness. This nation was not formed and based on concepts and doctrines put forth by non-Christian religions and philosophies, and such non-Christian teachings must not be allowed input into the continuation and development of America, or America will cease to continue in her development as God intended she should.

At the present time America is caught in the area of **[Hosea 4: 6-7],** where she is being destroyed because of a lack of knowledge that would prevent the destruction of the nation and her people. Reintroduction, pursuit, and practice of such essential knowledge would rekindle God's remembrance of her children, and reverse the processes and practices of sin and iniquity that has this great nation overwhelmed with shame and disgrace, **[2 Chronicles 7: 14]**.

It is apparent to all who have eyes to see, ears to hear, and minds with which to understand, that America is in desperate need of some permanent solutions to the problems and dilemmas we have burdened ourselves with: but we seem to lack the wherewithal, wisdom, knowledge, understanding, intelligence, and common sense, to deliver ourselves from our own stupidity.

But such has been the common lot of man who has, in his idiocy of disobedience and rebellion, excommunicated God and His Word of truth and absolutes and decided to do things his own way without God's counsel and direction down through history. Indeed has Shakespeare been correct in his summation of humanity, **"What fools ye mortals be"**.

America in her short life has already gone down the road of self destruction much to far by our own **[Romans 1: 30],**

"inventors of evil things" plus our indulgence's in evil things that were invented long before we came along. It is because of this "blind leading the blind" concept, and the blind followers being so stupid as to willingly follow the blind leaders, that we are witnessing today the positive growth and development of America coming to a screeching halt.

Indeed we are developing many advanced and clever material items that testify to the abilities God has designed in man, but the **spiritual** and **moral stability** on which the continuation of all these lesser things depend is rapidly being trash canned; **and the mortal immoral fools continue to be mortal immoral fools.** Once again we are reminded that **"God's thoughts and ways are higher than man's thoughts and ways as the heavens are above the earth", [Isaiah 55: 8-9].**

Man, with his inferior mentality, has a difficult time getting a grip on this as a Biblical absolute, and as a result has an equally difficult time adjusting to it. This is also true in Christendom. We are not perfect, we have our struggles, but our struggles are generally for maturity within God's truth, not against his Word of truth unto our own destruction. Of course there are exceptions. There will always be exceptions where man in his wishy, washy, unstable ways are concerned, where he is tossed about according to his various, constantly changing feelings and emotions.

This is referred to in **[Ephesians 4: 14]** as being as **"children, tossed to and fro, and carried about with every wind of doctrine, by the sleight of men, and cunning craftiness, whereby they lie in wait to deceive.** This seems to have a ring of *peer pressure* to it. It will always be this way until man completely surrenders to God and the counsel and direction of his word which never changes.

Personally I do not like the term "religion". It has somewhat of a generic implication and lacks the specifics that the Christian experience teaches and deserves, such as the **"doctrine of Christ", [Hebrews 6: 1], and the "Fruit of the Spirit", [Galatians 5: 23-23], etc.** In the early days of our nation when referred to, it would have been understood as the Christian religion or faith.

In our post-modern world, however, it includes everything from A to Z and has lost its meaning and value when searching for absolutes of truth. Now when it is used, we must emphasize the word "Christian" or risk the probability of being misunderstood as referring to, or at least including some other "religion".

There is a significant difference between religions whether or not people understand and except this difference. God established the difference, his people know the difference, and that certainly makes the difference, although we continue to have our difficulties in the process of developing and maturing.

The attempt to herd the Christians into the corrals of compliance to political correctness and not offending the anti-Bible, anti-Christ, element of society continues with separation of church and state and ACLU backing. Indeed, how terribly the mighty has fallen. May those who have been instrumental in initiating this abomination be swallowed up in their own pit of destruction: **[Psalms 2: 1-4], vs. 4, "He that sitteth in the heavens shall laugh: the Lord shall have them in derision". [Job 5: 6-7], "Although affliction cometh not forth of the dust, neither doth trouble spring out of the ground; Yet man is born unto trouble as the sparks fly upward". [Isaiah 50: 11], "Behold, all ye that compass yourselves about with sparks: walk in the light of your fire, and in the sparks that ye have kindled. This shall ye have of mine hand; ye shall lie**

down in sorrow". Thank God for his patience, love, forgiveness, and grace, etc, etc, etc, and certainly his counsel and word of correction and direction. Repentance forms the foundation for all of this.

God, through his Holy Spirit, is absolutely perfect in the transmission of his word and teaching, however, we as the receivers seem to have a rather difficult time with spiritual static in our receiving, understanding, and learning what God is sending. Thus do our struggles continue and we certainly need constant maintenance with upgrading on our mental receiving equipment. An important part of this is consistent, diligent study of the Word. This is the process by which the mind is renewed, **[Romans 12: 2], renewing the mind unto Bible conditioning and direction, and the heart is diligently kept and nurtured in righteousness, holiness, and purity with the issuing forth of life and life more abundantly, [Proverbs 4: 23].** Try it, you'll like it, it works wonders.

It does take considerable effort to accomplish spiritual growth and development. It isn't nearly as easy as existing as an idiot without purpose, discipline, and direction. However, with the inclusion of Biblically taught humility, the results and rewards make it all worthwhile, including accepting help when someone wants to give it. Resistance to correction seems to come natural to we proud humans, which is why we need discipline, teaching, and correction, beginning at a very young age. Unfortunately this doesn't always work out like it should, as it is becoming increasingly apparent that many who are responsible for such discipline, direction, and guidance, have they themselves never been instructed in, or learned, the art of administering what they are now expected to do, and responsible to accomplish.

The roots of this go to the beginning of the rejection of God and his standards. The more people rejected and neglected the input of God's principles in the past, the more unprincipled they became to the present. Unless this is corrected, the digression of obedience will continue on into the future with our nation and her people paying a horrible price for such stupidity. We have for some time been seeing the extensive evidence of this error and **lack of the knowledge of Biblical teaching with its absolutes, [Hosea 4:6].**

The farther away from God's influence people get, the more unprincipled they become. Thus, the more they neglected it, the more they resisted it, with the government also now discouraging such Biblical pursuits. Is it any wonder that so many of our young people go through broken homes, our educational systems, and still graduate from whatever school they graduate from dumber than a box of rocks, especially concerning their national heritage and Bible orientated spiritual matters on which their very life and future depends.

Thank God for the exceptions, we need more of them! But who's to blame for all this descending into idiocy when God created us in his own image and likeness? And somewhere within this "likeness" there is **an "excellency" [Job 4: 21], "that goes away, or went away, and we die, even without wisdom".**

We are to blame, for we have been extremely negligent in investing our time, efforts, and energies in the investigation and pursuit of this "excellency". For the most part we don't even know it exists and that it is yet available to us by God's amazing grace through Jesus our Lord. God's grace and patience is beyond our comprehension. While at the same time, our own ignorance and indifference to all the essentials is wreaking havoc with our own spiritual development. Once again I am reminded of Shakespeare's words, **"What fools ye mortals be"**!

Our challenge now is the "RESSURECTION OF EXCELLENCY" within us as individuals, revitalizing the inner man with an ancient, yet new and real, relatively unacknowledged truth that God is still with us and wants to dwell in our hearts with this "excellency" of glory of which we know nothing, and have experienced only a glimpse. What a challenge; and for the most of us, a completely new and unexplored frontier of which the Bible is our only source of information and revelation.

Explore this frontier at your own risk of finding joy unspeakable and full of glory, peace that passes all understanding, contentment of being, fulfillment of purpose, life and life more abundantly, and a multitude of other wonders that we in our little finite minds cannot even begin to comprehend.

God's thoughts are not our thoughts and his ways are not our ways. We can be very thankful for this. It would be very depressing to realize that we are the ultimate in our present state of mental and spiritual development with it being impossible to rise above our present state of being. That in itself is a depressing thought. Thank God for blessed deliverance. His thoughts and ways are a part of his likeness and the "excellency" he desires for us to embrace and attain to.

As undeserving as man is, what a glorious privilege God has granted us. Because God is love, he is compelled by that love to extend to us grace and goodness that we cannot understand. We must just accept it, and show our gratitude by returning that love to him and to one another in joyful obedience. I recall a story about a little colored lady giving a testimony, and using

[Psalms 103: 2], "Bless the Lord, Oh my soul, and forget not all his benefits". She misquoted it a little, but I am impressed by the truth she presented as only she could: **"Bless de Lawd, O my soul, and I gets all de benefits"**. It could not have been said any more beautiful, nor could it have been said any more correctly and I wonder if God didn't smile just a little when he heard it.

There must have been some angels giving high fives on that one, I don't know, I wasn't there. But I will never forget the story or the magnificent truth revealed in it. I don't know if the lady was highly educated or not, it makes no difference, she had tapped into God's excellency for intimacy of relationship with Him and that's all that mattered for her and for us all. He doesn't require that we be highly educated or successful by this worlds standards, but simply that we love him, and **[Mark 1: 15]**, **"Repent and believe his gospel unto obedience"**, **[Colossians 3: 2]**, **"Setting our affection on the things above and not on things on the earth"**.

The study of God's "excellency" certainly contains more than we could ever come up with in its description or content, but that should not keep us from extensive exploration and examination of what we can see of it, realizing that we will learn more as we proceed. In **Psalms** and **Proverbs** we find three things that are required to start building a foundation for study of this "excellency". They are; **wisdom, knowledge,** and **understanding.** As these have a direct bearing on the need of a sound Biblically informed and educated mind; I have included, for my own purposes and reasons, **"intelligence"** as another requirement that is desperately needed in our exploration of "excellency". We could very easily and accurately include common sense and discretion here. There may be others that you may wish to include for your own benefit and inspiration.

There are many instances where plain old fashioned **"common sense"** is appropriate and desperately needed for correct solutions to some of our problems. Indeed, all of these are vitally essential to the spiritual growth and maintenance of our lives as individuals and the process of the restoration of our nation, if indeed it is to be restored. Unfortunately these essentials have been in short supply and in some cases, non-existent for years, the result of which is the declining state of America. They are just as essential to the rebuilding of a single life, a marriage, family, even a church or governmental structure that has lost its direction for whatever reason.

It happens; churches are made of people and where ever you find people, you find problems, **[Job 5: 6-7], "Although affliction cometh not forth of the dust, neither doth trouble spring out of the ground; Yet man is born unto trouble, as the sparks fly upward"**. *Ve grow to soon old, un to late schmart.* Thank God there is a learning process and some, a few, not all, are availing themselves of it. Thank God for the provision of a mind that is able to think, reason, and learn, even though the process may at times be quite slow, but God is longsuffering and with patient endurance for which we all should be very thankful.

"Patience"; there is another vital quality of God's excellency that we would do well to study, pursue, and embrace as one of the essential **"things that accompany salvation"**, **[Hebrews 6: 9], "and always please God"**, **[John 8: 29]**. If you've got nothing else to do, work on patience. That will be a lifetime endeavor for most of us along with others, like **"forgiveness"** for instance, which will challenge you on a daily basis; not only in the forgiveness of others, but learning to forgive yourself, which can be a tough nut to crack but vitally essential to our individual and corporate well being.

You repent and know God has forgiven you, others have forgiven you, but place yourself under heavy condemnation because you won't forgive yourself. Your feelings and emotions get in the way and the devil takes advantage of them as he can manipulate them and you won't even know its happening; *unless you've been educated in this area.* Your feelings will lie to you and keep you in bondage to condemnation, *but your feelings have nothing to do with the matter;* **ITS GOD'S WORD THAT COUNTS,** it is what **"THUS SAITH THE LORD".** Remember this and rely on it.

You can never build your life on feelings and emotions that are like "unstable water" **[Genesis 49: 4].** God's word is the only foundation that never changes or wavers; you can build your eternity on it. **[Matthew 24: 35], "Heaven and earth shall pass away, but my words shall not pass away".** His Word, His Truth, is our blueprint and specifications for eternity; build your life on it, build your all on it and **"you shall never fall", [2 Peter 1: 10].**

God's Word is the foundation of the "Christian religion", It is the foundation, strength, stability, and direction for America; unfortunately, we have let our mooring slip and America's glory has turned into shame, **[Hosea 4: 7]. [Matthew 12: 30], "He that is not with me is against me; and he that gathereth not with me, scattereth abroad".**

How can we possibly be with him if we allow our "judges" to separate the church, the source of God's supply, counsel, and direction to the people, from the state, which is supposed to represent and assist in the spiritual education and development of the populace, thus providing direction and protection through the people for the benefit of the entire nation? We are seeing the dreadful results of this idiocy on our television screens every hour of every day, and increasing as the days go by.

[Job 4: 19-20], tells us that **"they that dwell in houses of clay, man, are destroyed from morning to evening: they perish forever without any regarding it"**. **[Jeremiah 12: 11]**, **"The whole land is desolate, because no man layeth it to heart"**, or regards, knows, what is happening to them. Indeed they do not have the knowledge to know, nor the intelligence to prevent their catastrophes which are presently heavy upon the land, **[Hosea 4: 6]**. America has become as a blind man, groping in the darkness.

No intelligent questions are asked, thus no intelligent answers are sought as needed; consequently none are found, and man continues in his mode of self destruction. It is utterly amazing how this man that God created to be so intelligent has become so degraded, ignorant, and overbearingly stupid, and our nation is suffering as a result.

Thank God for the minority, the few, the exceptions who have embraced what God has provided for all men and are living it. But there is still hope for whosoever will **"choose life and blessing rather than remaining under the curse of death and additional curses simply because they refuse to obey God's counsel to** *choose life and blessing so that BOTH they and their seed, descendents,* **and their nation may live"**, **[Deu. 30: 19]**.

It's an amazing thing, this choosing life according to what God determines life to be instead of the struggles of existence buried under waves of the foolishness, folly, and failures that man interprets as life. This is an existence of deceptions without God and his counsel for direction, purpose, and fulfillment.

This life that God desires for us is synonymous with the excellency contained in his likeness. All three of these things; life, excellency, and his likeness, because of who they are contained in and proceed from, are worthy of whatever time, effort, thought, and energy we can put into them for their renewal, reclamation, or resurrection. This is blessing de Lawd with all our souls, and we gets all de benefits. What a beautiful truth, even though it is contained in a misquotation. I don't know if this is a true accounting of an actual event or not, but regardless, it portrays a spiritual condition of mentality that we could all use more of, **to bless the Lord with all our souls; to live and move and have our being in him, [Acts 17: 28]**. This is life and life more abundantly, manifesting his "excellency" within us.

"Wisdom", what an interesting subject it is. It's another one of those things without which we can only hope to exist. **[Psalms 111: 10], "The fear,** *reverence,* **of the Lord is the beginning of wisdom".** There is a question in my mind here as to the usage of the word "fear" supplied by the translators instead of "reverencing" in this application. I am certainly not questioning the authority and accuracy of the Bible and its truth; however it does make me wonder about the "wisdom" of the translators in the use of the word "fear". It was translated in a different time and age when the understanding of the word may have been a bit different than that of our post-modern era.

Today the general understanding of the word seems to be afraid, frightened, scared, etc. At any rate it has a certain fearful connotation to it that does not fit in well with many scriptures. We get a better understanding of the improper use of the word in relation to God when we consider the fact that "God is love" and we have been commanded to "love " or reverence him, not fear him **[John 4: 18], "There is no fear in love; but perfect love casteth out fear: because fear hath torment. He that "feareth" is not made perfect in love".**

It would be impossible to have the intimacy of a love relationship with God and be frightened and afraid of him at the same time. This intimacy with him is based on our loving obedience to God. **[John 14: 15], "If you love me, keep my commandments.** Jesus did not die so that we might have a limited knowledge of the Word and a casual acquaintance with God, but that we might have a relationship of intimacy with our Lord.

It is not difficult to understand God's perfect love for us, after all, he is God, but it is our love for him that we need to be concerned about and work on unto perfection. If there is any trouble between us and God, it will come from our discrepancy, God doesn't have any. **[Matthew 22: 37], "Jesus said unto him, Thou shalt love the Lord thy God, *not fear*, with all thy heart, and with all thy soul, and with all thy mind".**

Personally, I enjoy an intimacy of love relationship with God. He is my friend in the deepest sense who has redeemed me and reconciled me back to himself so we might also walk and talk together and reason together as he teaches me how to have thoughts like his thoughts, so my ways may become at least, more like his ways. It seems like I have a long way to go, but our majestic God who is the God of love, is also the God of patience, longsuffering, and amazing grace. However, don't overlook the fact that where sin is involved, our God of love is also a God of hate. You never hear anything about this Godly attribute of the hatred of sin, iniquity, every false way, etc, etc, but there are several scriptures pertaining to this which is an attitude toward sin, abominations, and detestable things we would do well to adopt.

Patience is one of his ways I'm still kind of short on, there are others also. When we exit this world, our ways may well still be imperfect but our desires for perfection can be perfect and assist us in the development of perfecting our ways while we are still here. **[Romans 2: 7, 10], "To them who by patient continuance in well doing seek for glory and honour and immortality, eternal life". Vs. 10, "But glory, honour, and peace, to every man that worketh good, to the Jew first, and also to the Gentile".**

It may well be that the "fear" concept concerning a repentant sinner is quite justified as this person does not know, as yet, what it is to "reverence and love" God. Nor is there any understanding of the love God has for them; I'm not sure any of us really understand the extent of this. Getting grounded in this as a new Christian generally takes time, how much time depends on the quality of teaching and their willingness to receive it.

I have found that the "fear factor" is quite deeply entrenched in the teachings of Christendom. Reverencing is hardly ever mentioned anymore. Initially, fear may bring the sinner to his knees in repentance as an introduction to wisdom with a relationship of reverencing and love for the Holy Spirit to teach and develop along the way. If this reverencing meaning of fear is not introduced and explained to the new convert, they will continue in their relationship with God based on the negative side of fear until such time as God helps them to realize, it is their love he desires, not fear. **Matthew 22:37-40].**

It is, after all, the reverencing of God that is the beginning of wisdom. Now how about the continuation of development and growth of wisdom? We've got the beginning. Now what? Where do we go from here? How about diligence in patient continuation in learning and seeking God, **[Hebrews 11: 6]** for studying, loving, delighting, meditation, etc, for the expanding of our horizons of wisdom, knowledge, and understanding? We've just gotten started on our journey and hunt for the

treasures to be found in God's Word. **[1 Peter 1: 13],
"Wherefore gird up the loins of your mind, be sober, and
hope for the end for the grace that is brought unto you at
the revelation of Jesus Christ".**

NOTES

IX.

Bible Consciousness

Bible consciousness: Making oneself aware of how scripture applies to normal everyday functions, beginning with the mentality, thoughts and thinking, in relationship to conversation, conduct and activities! In making oneself "aware" of Biblical concepts of truth and absolutes, we obviously must conclude that considerable time invested in study, **[2 Timothy 2: 15]**, delighting in and meditation in the Word, **[Psalms 1: 2]**, with in-depth thinking, thought, and concentration, **[Philippians 4: 6-9],** are necessary.

There are scriptures that pertain directly to those psychological activities of our thinking capabilities, such as **[Romans 12:2]**, the **"renewing of the mind"** for the explicit purpose of being delivered from the worldly influences and conditioning and following Godly principles, standards, and values.

God has commanded this for the purpose of restructuring and redirecting of the mind to establish that which is **commensurate with God's thoughts and ways, [Isaiah 55:7-9]**, **"and the reverencing of God and the working of righteousness that is acceptable to Him", [Acts 10:35].** [Philippians 4:8], **"Finally, brethren, whatsoever things are true, whatsoever things are honest, whatsoever things are just, whatsoever things are pure, whatsoever things are lovely, whatsoever things are of good report; if there be any virtue, if there be any praise, think on these things".** Verses 7 and 9 of this chapter give us full assurance of God being with us and keeping us if we follow his commands and counsel. We must use wisdom, knowledge, and understanding in determining the "things" mentioned in **4:8,** searching them out and **studying them diligently.**

Concerning righteousness; let's take a look at Webster's Dictionary to get a sense of direction concerning what it means. Acting rightly: upright, according to what is right! What is right by God's standards is considerably above and superior to man's ideas of rightness, and God's standards must prevail or all is lost. Unfortunately we live in a society where humanistic relativity has terribly distorted the concept of right versus wrong which leaves Webster's definition somewhat at loose ends with considerable argument as to what it really means.

After all, the secular humanists tell us well, what is wrong for you may be alright for me; the main problem with that is they go by the "if it feels good do it" idea, which is one of the strongest "gates of hell" the devil has ever raised against mankind. So everything is approved and right by however they feel and they will judge you and your ideas on the basis of how they feel, which may be one way today and a totally different way tomorrow, but never good or correct.

I can't help but wonder, when did this bunch of brain dead imbeciles with their promotion of confusion and chaos get to take over as authorities on what is right versus what is wrong and get established to make policy for America? As for me, I'll go with God's principles of truth and absolutes as set forth in his Word regardless who it offends or the extent of the violation of "political correctness".

This makes them extremely undependable, unreliable, and unacceptable, diversifying toward the demands of their feelings and emotions which are in a constant state of change. They will find out, too late, that God has very specifically established what is right versus wrong, good versus evil for all men. God has established some "behavioral traffic lights" for societies to live by which are obligatory on all, and we are to exercise ourselves to the maintaining of our conduct within their guidelines.

What man determines as good or evil, legal versus illegal has no bearing on God's established principles of righteousness versus unrighteousness. It is not what you or I think that counts, it is what, "thus saith the Lord" and he is not about to change his mind, concepts, and agenda simply because man in his ignorance and arrogance chooses to oppose and disagree with him regardless of who they are or how important they think they are or esteem themselves to be.

We are living in an extended period of time when, with a few exceptions, Bible Consciousness is at an extremely low ebb to virtually non-existent. This applies to the masses of humanity among whom there are the few exceptions who have **[Colossians 3:2], "Set their affections on things above, and not on things on the earth".** These "exceptions" are the members of the **[Matthew 16: 18]** church that Jesus is building against which, **"the gates of hell shall not prevail".**

The sad lack of Bible Consciousness is not necessarily the direct result of any one decision made by anyone to reject the Word. This is a result of an extremely slow growing, encroaching deception that arises, not necessarily out of intended rejection, but out of continual, distracting, unintentional neglect of **[Matthew 6:33], "seeking first the kingdom of God and his righteousness, [Deuteronomy 28:47], serving the Lord thy God with joyfulness and gladness of heart for the abundance of all things".**

This neglect, intentional or unintentional, has the continuing results of distracting our Bible conditioned affections and getting them "sidetracked" as this world has a multitude of desirable, interesting, fun, important, etc things to do that keep us sidetracked. Many of these things though important from a feeling and emotion standpoint, from a wisdom and discretion point of view are not necessarily essential and neither **"accompany nor enrich our salvation"**, **[Hebrews 6:9]**. Because of their non-essential status they may well be of a nature that **"adds nothing to us" [Galatians 2: 6],** and can not be classified among those things that have to do with **"doing always those things that please God", [John 8: 29].**

At this time we need to make a distinction between the legitimate things which can be enjoyed while we can still remain with our affection firmly set on the things above, and are aware of and guard against the things that destroy those affections. A big difference arises as we use what God has lovingly provided for us by whatever means he chooses and express our gratitude for them, keeping them in their place of importance and not allowing them to become the priorities in our lives, but maintaining our **"seeking first the kingdom of God and his righteousness", [Matthew 6: 33].**

When things, basically but not limited to material, are desired to the point they achieve godlike status, elevating our wants over our needs, our affection has been derailed, and we need an overhaul "renewing" of our minds as to what is essential and what is not, what is pleasing to God and what isn't. As a Christian, if we have our head screwed on straight, we will desire and pursue; **"doing those things that always please God", [John 8: 29],** the **"fearing, or reverencing God, and the working of righteousness", [Acts 10: 32].**

If we don't have our affection focused properly by God's standards and values, we are of the crowd that **"honors God with the lips, but the heart is far from Him, [Matthew 15:8],** causing not only problems for ourselves, but everyone around us and are in desperate need of God's counsel for correction and help. There are certainly reasons for such commands, directions, and admonishments from God's Word such as being **"sober and vigilant", [1 Peter 5:8],** concerning Biblical counsel and direction in all areas of life.

If regarded, taken to heart, obeyed, call it what you will, they are designed to deliver us from our own self imposed ignorance and stupidity of victimizing ourselves with disobedience; or **"choosing death and cursing, [Deuteronomy 30:19], "which we equally and as ignorantly pass on to our posterity"**.

The neglect mentioned is due to not having a vision of the value of God's counsel of righteousness for deliverance from sin and glorifying God. This neglect results in violating **[Psalms 1: 2]**, not delighting in God's Word and meditating in it day and night.

Man, because of his sinful nature, has a strong tendency to gravitate toward whatever he sees as contributing to his personal interests, even if those interests are misled and erroneous. We see this manifested quite forcefully in a demand for "rights", be they civil, constitutional, unalienable or whatever, to do whatever one wants to do regardless of who it injures.

This psychological, gravitational pull of an evil heart conditioned with worldly thoughts that are contrary to God's thoughts that establish ways that are contrary to God's ways is what is simply known as sin. Bible awareness and consciousness teaches, and convicts, which is uncomfortable with this type of attitude and conduct, which is why the selfish, self centered soul rejects and denies any value connected to God's Word. Consequently these misled souls seek value in the things of earth that are contrary to God's thoughts and ways, **"the things above"**, **[Colossians 3:2]**, and continue to revel in their earth bound abominations.

This neglect of **"exercising ourselves unto Godliness"**, **[1 Timothy 4:7],** and its destructive results is precisely why we must avail ourselves of the Holy Spirit for considerable "one on one" teaching and revelation of what God wants us to learn and apply for the **"prosperity of the soul"**, **[3 John :2]**. With the deceptive encroachment of this neglect, intentional or unintentional, we slowly but assuredly slip into a **"lack of knowledge" [Hosea 4:6],** condition where destruction waits to ambush us.

This whole process is so insidious and subtle that it takes shape and becomes entrenched without any awareness for **"regarding it or laying it to heart" [Job 4: 20; Jeremiah 12:11],** with many even enjoying it, spending much time, effort, and finances to pursue it for additional indulgences in the extremely fickle and momentary pleasures of sin.

Then when trouble comes as a result we hear the phrase "Where did we go wrong", Why did God allow this to happen? We can see, finally, that there are problems and we wring our hands and scratch or heads as we as we wonder how these things got so anchored in our lives. We wander around in confusion trying to find something or someone to blame as the confusion continues over a solution for correction to the dilemma's we have caused by our stupidity and ignorance, which of course we would never admit to.

As a result, the government makes new laws and appoints more committees to investigate something they know nothing about and will deny even exists. The church in response invents more programs consisting of seemingly endless spiritual exercises. This is done for activity involvement and hope that somehow these churchy calisthenics will solve the existing problems and prevent any additional dilemma's we devise and endure through our **"lack of knowledge"**, **[Hosea 4: 6; Matthew 15: 8-9; Mark 7: 6-7; Isaiah 29: 13-16]**.

It seems that we are witnessing a growing nervousness among the anti-Bible, anti-Christian segment of our American society including our so called leaders, politicians, judges, etc. They have had their way at the helm of our nation for several decades and things continue to get worse and their blaming each other has provided no solutions to our ever increasing dilemmas.

Neither has the science that was once proclaimed as the salvation to our rising problems done what was claimed it would do. Over the last 50-60 years of our traditional leadership, things have very steadily and rapidly gotten worse nation wide, and all our leadership can do is argue among themselves as to the cause and blame someone else with still no forth coming solutions. But then it can't be expected for earthly minded creatures to come up with spiritual solutions to spiritual problems, which is exactly what America is faced with.

Disobedience and rebellion against God is a spiritual problem and will cause multitudes of physiological and physical problems, including a variety of diseases, which will in turn adversely affect every part of our nation. This can only be solved by the spiritual remedy of obedience, **[2 Chronicles 7:14]**. Without elaborating on it as found in this scripture, we find it in essence repeated in **[Mark 1:15],** stated in much briefer terms, **"Repent and believe the gospel".** It must be understood here that it is speaking of **"believing the gospel *unto obedience*",** not just believing unto a shallow acknowledgement of its existence.

You can read it over and over, hear it time and time again, but it only has effect when it is activated within our hearts, and that with willing, purposeful, diligence; **[James 1: 22], "But be ye doers of the word, and not hearers of the word only, deceiving your own selves.**

There is no doubt that an extreme emphasis must be placed on being a "doer" of the word, not just a hearer or reader, but a diligent student. Being a diligent doer involves a lot more than the majority of us have ever been taught and certainly involves much more than just attending church and Sunday School for attendance sake.

However, very few ever seemed to develop the zeal to excel in the training needed to really roll up their sleeves and proclaim the gospel of Jesus Christ. They just settled into a defensive posture and continued to go to church and Sunday School as traditionally required, expected, and accepted as sufficient, and I must admit I was no exception.

So as we continued in our traditions and customs, with their sometimes questionable results, the secular humanists, evolutionists, and any other anti-Christian groups and individuals made their advances against the Christian religion and the battle has been going on with increasing intensity on the opposition's part. Here is a quote from a sermon text of Dr. D. James Kennedy, **"The best lack all conviction, while the worst are full of passionate intensity".** It would certainly seem that we are long overdue to **"stir up ourselves to take hold of God" [Isaiah 64: 7].**

I wonder if there are any of us that really can get a grasp of the seriousness of what we are challenged with in the proclamation of this glorious gospel of truth and deliverance from sin. It is difficult for us from the safety and comfort of our American experience, to get an appreciation for the oppressions of the dear ones who have truly suffered and died to preserve this spiritual heritage that has been delivered to us.

In our lethargy, neglect and lack of attention to our calling and spiritual responsibilities, we have let much of it slip through our fingers by the ridiculous opposition we have allowed to deter us. Our **"lack of conviction"** is our own fault; we can't even blame that on the devil, although as usual, we will try to find some thing or some one else to use as a scapegoat.

I'm afraid we have not been as Bible conscious as we should have been over the years, but basically we have just gotten into it as deep as we were led by those who led us only as deep as they were taught and led. For a bunch of people who should be able to **reclaim God's image and likeness through the blood of Jesus for dominion over the works of God's hands, [Psalms 8:6],** we haven't done very good.

As a matter of fact we have done pretty much the same thing Adam did in the abdication of his God given authority. We really don't have much to cry about as we have stood on the sidelines and let this aggressive, hostile takeover of our government and nation proceed. May God in his mercy forgive us for our failure **"to dress and to keep", [Genesis 2: 15],** this marvelous land he gave us.

There is no doubt that, **[2 Corinthians 10: 4-5], "the weapons of our warfare are not carnal, but mighty through God to the pulling down of strongholds; Casting down imaginations, and every high thing that exalts itself against the knowledge of God, and bringing into captivity every thought to the obedience of Christ"**. *Our main problem seems to be that we have not wisely used our time to involve ourselves in the "perfect practice" needed to gain proficiency in the use of our "spiritual weapons". Not only do we need this perfect practice, we need to get a renewed knowledge of what these weapons are and a revitalized confidence in their ability to accomplish the results required. This depends, however, on our commitment to their proper use. The problem has never been with the weapons, but with an undeveloped ability to know them intimately and wisely for their proper use to accomplish that for which they were intended and provided.*

"These weapons, not being carnal, but mighty through God to the tearing down of strongholds", [2 Corinthians 10:4], should be a natural extension of our total being in Christ. When we move, they move as one with us, maintaining a condition of constant **"soberness and vigilance", [1 Peter 5:8];** *soberness* and *vigilance* themselves being two of our weapons. Man's problem is that he is to drawn away, distracted, of "his own lust" for the fun, games, glitz, glamour, and glory of the world he lives in to take time to **"think on these things" of [Philippians 4: 7-9],** and reap the benefits of them, but cursed for his neglect of them.

We have a bunch of strongholds and "gates of hell" opposing the gospel in our nation and society today, and we are doing a lousy job of pulling them down; ***what is our problem?*** The church is experiencing many of the same problems the world is experiencing and if we can't keep the church, the redeemed community of Christ, on course with the instruction manual at out fingertips, how in heavens name can we ever hope to pull down the strongholds of the world that are formed against us?

As sad as it is, I'm afraid the churches have formed many of their own "gates of hell" that are prevailing against them. It looks like a good time to check our weapons to see if they are operational or if their all corroded up from lack of use or if we even know what they are anymore, and be honest in an assessment of our proficiency in the use of them as God intended we should be.

I have heard it said that "practice makes perfect", then I heard an upgrading of that old saying that made real sense to me but presented a much larger challenge of deciding what it was going to involve to make it all work, **"perfect practice makes perfect"**. I believe it was Vince Lombardi who was a famous, highly successful coach of the Green Bay Packers who was credited for that bit of wisdom and knowledge. Maybe we are lacking in some perfect practice sessions and pursuits or the people qualified to teach them. Unfortunately and quite subtlety we have been, to some extent, diverted from "what thus saith the Lord" to what thus saith man with to much **[Matthew 15: 9; Mark 7:7], "teaching for doctrines the commandments of men"**.

Now I had to decide what "perfect practice" consisted of, especially from a spiritual perspective. I hadn't thought of this but a few moments until the master teacher of the universe brought something "to my remembrance" which made for some sound reasoning to me and simply said, "personalize it", with the additional thought; "practice what you preach, the things you've written". This brought me to **[Deuteronomy 10:12-13], "And now, *Darold*, what doth the Lord thy God require of thee, but to fear the Lord thy God, to walk in *all* his ways,** and to love him, and to serve the Lord thy God with all thy heart and with all thy soul, To keep the commandments of the Lord, and his statutes, which I command thee this day for thy good".

Statutes, commandments, and laws, translate into *God's Word* for those that have a hard time with words such as commandments, statutes, law, etc, that are high centered on grace, sitting and just spinning their spiritual wheels, and can't get beyond it to embrace **"the things that accompany salvation, [Hebrews 6:9]** and **"the things that always please God", [John 8:29]**. However, I am extremely thankful for the "amazing grace" that sustains and keeps me in my times of failure and lack; but we won't go there.

Allow me to do a bit of paraphrasing of **[Matthew 23:23]** with which you may or may not agree, it makes no difference, it works for me. **"Woe unto you, scribes and Pharisees, hypocrites, slackers, lethargic, insincere, unknowledgeable! For ye claim grace, grace, and grace upon grace to hide and cover your waywardness and disobedience, and have omitted the weightier matters of God's word, repentance, obedience, faith, judgment, mercy, forgiveness, the fruit of the spirit, etc, etc, etc. These ye ought to have done, and do, and not to leave the other undone. For it is the doers of the word, not the hearers only, who fear the Lord and worketh righteousness that are justified and accepted with the Lord our God, for it is in him that we live and move and have our being, certainly with a healthy, saving application of God's grace on his part, but with at least an equal amount of God pleasing obedience on our part which must begin with a soul depth repentance of sin and believing the gospel. [Romans 6:17-20], verse 19, "for as ye have yielded your members servants to uncleanness and iniquity unto iniquity; even so now yield your members servants to righteousness unto holiness". [Ephesians 2: 1-13], "BUT GOD"!

Obedience goes way beyond pulling a warm fuzzy blanket of grace around you to get spiritually comfortable in an attempt to calm your anxieties, but is given to keep and maintain us in our spiritual battles when we stumble and fall, to lift us up, dust us off, and get us going again, all to the glory and honour of God. [John 8:29], "And he that sent me is with me, the Father hath not left me alone; FOR I DO ALWAYS THOSE THINGS THAT PLEASE HIM". [Philippians 2:5-8], vs. 8,"he humbled himself and became OBEDIENT unto death, even the death of the cross".

It does seem that **"obedience unto the good works ordained by God" [Ephesians 2: 10],** is quite a commendable objective to pursue for attainment in our everyday Christian living. This undoubtedly has much to do with our attitudes, which we are continually challenged to keep Biblically in check and on track. Some times we meet the challenge, sometimes we don't, but in the process we gain half a step in our spiritual journey.

Regardless, in our daily struggles, through our successes and failures, the sustaining grace of God remains sufficient to see us through our frailties as we **"forget those things which are behind, reach forth to those things which are before and press on, in willing, joyful, obedience, to the high calling of God in Christ Jesus",** [Philippians 3: 13-14]. [1 Peter 1:13], **"Wherefore gird up the loins of your mind, be sober, and hope to the end for the grace that is to be brought unto you at the revelation of Jesus Christ".**

Throughout the years in my observations of humanity, I have seen nothing in their scheming, planning, conniving, whatever, that even remotely begins to approach or compare with that which God has provided for our temporal and eternal security. God has equipped and enabled man to accomplish some great, grand, and noble things, but in a few years they too succumb to the elements of time. We see them in various degrees of decay and demise **"where moth and rust, stupidity and ignorance, has corrupted and brought them to ruin"** if they were of material origin.

If they happened to be of mental, psychological composition, all that was needed for their end was for someone of greater stature to change their mind and impose different, not necessarily better, ideas and concepts. These generally held somewhat firm until someone else rose to the podium of power, possibly a different political party; then everything changed again. Man has come up with nothing of stability and value within his own concoctions and conjuring that he can trust his future to.

Man in his vacillating, relative nature provides nothing on which he himself can depend for stability and certainty. Even our grand and beautiful America, once a noble and majestic nation, *is now suffering shame and disgrace at the hands of ignorance and stupidity* **"that have cast God aside and despised his Word", [Isaiah 5: 24].** In all this, that ignorance and stupidity has not the wherewithal to exercise the wisdom and intelligence to recant, repent, and to reinstate God to his rightful position of supreme Commander and Chief, Lord of All over our nation such as is commanded in **[2 Chronicles 7: 14]**, **"If my people, which are called by my name, shall humble themselves, and pray, and seek my face, and turn from their wicked ways; then I will hear from heaven, and forgive their sin, and will heal their land".**

This is stated again in a much more condensed, precise manner in **[Mark 1: 15], "The time is fulfilled, and the kingdom of heaven is at hand: REPENT YE, AND BELIEVE THE GOSPEL"**. This is going to take considerable **[1 Peter 1: 13], "girding up the loins of your minds"** for study and meditation of Biblical truths and absolutes unto diligence in obedience. This is something the world we live in knows nothing about. We do, as Christians, have life and life more abundantly in a realm far removed from this world as we learn to think the way God thinks so our thoughts are as His thoughts, and our ways conform to His ways.

Mankind must revive his Bible consciousness as his priority for direction and purpose or perish. He has no other choice but to continue in his self imposed destruction and annihilation, his choice of death and cursing, in rejection and denial of God's direction of life and blessing, **[Deuteronomy 30: 19]**.

Perhaps this is what prompted God to make the statement in **[Hosea 5: 15], "I will go and return to my place, till they acknowledge their offence, and seek my face: in their affliction they will seek me early"**. It would seem that America has not suffered sufficient affliction as yet to turn her mind away from her sin and iniquity and turn to God and seek His face. Being blind to God's goodness, America is also blind to his correction for direction and purpose. What a shame America, and the world, continues to **"despise the riches of God's goodness, forbearance, and longsuffering; not having the intelligence to know that the Goodness of God leads to repentance"**, **[Romans 2: 4]**. Indeed, as William Shakespeare said, **"What fools ye mortals be"**.

NOTES

www.ingramcontent.com/pod-product-compliance
Lightning Source LLC
Chambersburg PA
CBHW051439290426
44109CB00016B/1614